The
Garland Library
of
War and Peace

The
Garland Library
of
War and Peace

Under the General Editorship of
Blanche Wiesen Cook, *John Jay College*, C.U.N.Y.
Sandi E. Cooper, *Richmond College*, C.U.N.Y.
Charles Chatfield, *Wittenberg University*

The Legal Position of War
Changes in Its Practice
and Theory from Plato to Vattel

by

William Ballis

with a new introduction
for the Garland Edition by
Wayne K. Patterson

Garland Publishing, Inc., New York & London
1973

The new introduction for this
Garland Library Edition is Copyright © 1973, by
Garland Publishing Inc.

———————

———————

Library of Congress Cataloging in Publication Data

Ballis, William Belcher, 1908-
  The legal position of war.

  (The Garland library of war and peace)
  Originally presented as the author's thesis,
University of Chicago.
  Bibliography: p.
  1. War (International law)--History. I. Title.
II. Series.
JX4508.B33 1973   341.6   75-147596
ISBN 0-8240-0357-8

Printed in the United States of America

Introduction

Organized around the notion that war becomes right (or, perhaps, less wrong) if waged under certain conditions, Dr. Ballis examines the development of Western international law and its relation to war from Ancient Greece to the eighteenth century. His presentation falls into a discussion of five problems: whether a distinction should be made between types of enemies; whether a war should begin by a formal declaration; whether and how a war should be judged as just or unjust; whether neutralism should be permitted; whether time and place restrictions on the waging of war are proper.

While several of these categories might seem to pale into insignificance in the context of modern international politics, nevertheless a closer examination suggests that such is not the case despite changing times and circumstances.

It is instructive to note that Western writers on international law from Plato forward have divided the world into "civilized" and "uncivilized" peoples, not unlike the Chinese system of classification. Indeed, until the Renaissance, wars were considered "just" if waged against "inferior" peoples (such as Infidels and the natives of Asia and the Americas) and the rules of warfare could be relaxed in these cases. The human-

5

ism of the Renaissance ended this theoretical distinction between "lawful" peoples and those "beyond the pale of the law." Unfortunately, the dictates of aggression and racism in contemporary international relations has given the lie to those who would argue that practice and theory are one.

The evolution of the concept of a just or unjust war is another consideration of the author which is of abiding interest. In Roman times, a war was just if it was declared. During the Middle Ages, a war was just if it was declared by the Pope. By the Reformation, the influence of Machiavelli and the age of imperialism and nationalism defined a just war as one undertaken for reasons of state. The existence of a double standard is useful for nations which seek to justify their wars as just by labeling their enemies as "bandits" or "international outlaws."

A final point which merits attention is that of the propriety or impropriety of declaring war. From the times of Greece and Rome in which heralds were used to notify civilized foes (a procedure deemed unnecessary for uncivilized foes) to the use of the printed document of more recent vintage, the traditional dichotomy between civilized and barbarian seems once more to be preserved. An interesting sidelight appears in the declaration of war issue because of the relation to domestic politics in which the recent (and not so recent) history of the United States is an example.

This book is perhaps most useful for showing how

INTRODUCTION

much legal thinking has changed from the time of the ancients to the eighteenth century. When this is combined with the reader's knowledge of modern history, more importantly perhaps, we can see how much legal practice *has remained the same, and the dualistic nature of words and deeds in the international arena remains intact.*

Wayne K. Patterson

with Hilary Conroy

Colloquium in Diplomacy
and Peacekeeping
University of Pennsylvania

THE LEGAL POSITION OF WAR: CHANGES IN ITS
PRACTICE AND THEORY FROM PLATO TO VATTEL

THE LEGAL POSITION OF WAR: CHANGES IN ITS PRACTICE AND THEORY FROM PLATO TO VATTEL

BY

WILLIAM BALLIS, PH.D.

Instructor in Political Science, The University of Chicago

THE HAGUE
MARTINUS NIJHOFF
1937

PREFACE

The problem of the legal position of war is not confined within the limits of any one historical epoch. Questions relating to the problem will no doubt arise as long as wars are waged between nations. They are not questions involving the international law of the conduct of war, but those which concern the legality or illegality of commencing war. It is this particular aspect of the problem of war that is considered in this study. The present work is not an investigation into the ethics of war, but an historical analysis of some of the legal issues which confront states contemplating participation or non-participation in war. While this book ends with the nineteenth century, the author hopes that it will contribute something to the clarification of the present problem of controlling war through international law.

Most of the recent works on this subject, written by such students as Vanderpol with his monumental La Doctrine Scolastique du Droit de la Guerre, Sturzo with his profound International Community and the Right of War and Regout with his provocative La Doctrine de la Guerre Juste de Saint Augustin à Nos Jours, have been written with emphasis on the doctrines of mediaeval churchmen. Although the contributions of the scholastics on this question have been very significant in the history of the subject, they are somewhat restricted by the political and ecclesiastical setting in which they were offered. While *the author wishes to acknowledge his indebtedness to the works of Vanderpol, Sturzo and Regout for their excellent analyses of the doctrines on war, he has found them somewhat insufficient for the investigator in international law. Because their interests are religious rather than legal, they have not interpreted the writings of the churchmen from the conceptual basis of international law. With the exception of Sturzo, they have confined their research mainly to the works of the churchmen and have omitted the earlier contributions of the Greeks and Romans and many of the successive works of the Renaissance Humanists and Reformers, as well as of the classics of the professional international law writers, all of which form the body of this book.*

One of the most pleasant tasks in the writing of a preface is to acknowledge the assistance which has been given to the author by his former teachers, colleagues, and friends. To them he wishes to express his obligation and thanks for many hours of lectures, seminars, and private conversations which have aided him in formulating his ideas more clearly and in directing his research more pointedly. Whatever errors and omissions are present in this work reflect only the misapplication by the author of advice and counsel of these generous people. Particular acknowledgment of gratitude must be given to two people. To Professor Quincy Wright, the author desires to pay homage and offer thanks for having suggested this study and for having supervised and encouraged it through all its stages. And to the author's wife who has helped him in numerous ways, he would like to express here his deepest obligation.

TABLE OF CONTENTS

INTRODUCTION

War has been primarily a technical matter — the use of weapons to accomplish political, economic, and military purposes. But in all civilizations, even among primitive people, war has had a legal aspect. The customs of primitive people have recognized that, if waged under certain circumstances, and with certain methods, war was right; while under other circumstances and with other methods, it was wrong. The customs of civilized people pertaining to war have been rationalized by philosophers, statesmen, and jurists in the discussion of the "legal position of war". The statement that war has a legal position implies the existence of a body of international law. While not until the sixteenth century in western Europe has there been a systematic literature of this subject, there is ample evidence to show that statesmen have recognized the existence of legal principles governing the relations between organized peoples.

It is proposed to examine the legal position of war in the ancient, mediaeval, and the early modern periods of the history of western Europe. While definitions of war [1] and international law might easily

---

[1] On the various definitions of war, cf. Clyde Eagleton, "The Attempt to Define War", *International Conciliation*, June 1933, Number 291 (New York: Carnegie Endowment for International Peace); Quincy Wright, "Changes in the Conception of War", *American Journal of International Law*, XVIII (1924), 755–67.

occupy much space, it will perhaps be sufficient to define war as the condition when public armed forces may properly be used between states, and international law, as a body of rules and principles governing the relations of states with each other. Such rules and principles have dealt with war in two types of law. The first, *jus ad bellum* (the law into war), comprises the law relating to commencing war; the second, *jus in bello* (the law in war), covers the law concerning the conduct of war [1]. The first type alone will be considered in this study. Within this type of the law of war are found the following problems:

1. With whom is it proper to wage war? Usually peoples of the same race and culture wage war under different circumstances and perhaps with different methods when they are fighting each other than when they are fighting with a different race and a different culture. The law often appears to make a "distinction between peoples with respect to war".

2. How should war be commenced? Often a formal "declaration of war" has been insisted upon.

3. What circumstances justify resort to war? Are there "just and unjust wars", or as some writers call them, "just and unjust causes of war"?

4. What is the appropriate attitude of non-participants? Should they be entirely neutral or should they intervene? Are there circumstances where they must join one side?

5. Where and when is waging war proper? Often

---

[1] Cf. Robert Regout, S. J., *La Doctrine de la Guerre Juste de Saint Augustin à nos Jours* (Paris: A. Pedone, 1935), p. 16.

hostilities have been forbidden in respect to time and place.

These problems, it must be noted here, were not made arbitrarily by the present writer but have developed in the practice of states and appear in the works of writers on the subject of war. These five sets of problems have been taken as the basis for the present investigation of the early practice and theory of the legal position of war.

The "distinction between peoples with respect to war", as it has been drawn in different periods and on different occasions, has been founded on the fact that peoples are different as to race, language, custom, religion, etc. Such a difference has often afforded a justification for waging war. Furthermore, once such a war has been commenced, rules for waging it, may be followed which are different from those which would be applied if the war were between peoples of the same race, language, etc. An interesting case in point is to be found in the recent Italian–Ethiopian dispute. In a lengthy memorandum presented to the Council of the League of Nations on September 4, 1935, the Italian representative, Baron Aloisi, implied such a "distinction between peoples with respect to war". The Italian memorandum charged the Ethiopians with slavery, emasculation of men and boys, and cannibalism and other barbaric practices [1]. Ethiopia, according to the

---

[1] "It is well known that it is the Ethiopian practice to cut off the sexual organs of the wounded or captured enemy, and treat these as trophies. Not only conquered warriors but also boys and infants are subject to emasculation. . . .

"Another atrocity known to be practiced is cannibalism for

Italian Government, was not worthy of statehood in the family of nations because Ethiopia had not brought herself up to the level of civilization of the world [1]. Ethiopia through her barbaric practices had placed herself beyond the "pale" of international law. Modern international law then could not be applied in this instance, according to the Italians, and thus legalistically they were not violating international agreements by attacking Ethiopia. Because the Ethiopians were "uncivilized", "different with respect to people", the Italians sought to justify themselves for their invasion.

The "distinction between peoples with respect to war" was also evident in the Sino–Japanese dispute of 1931–33. When the Japanese were carrying on military operations against the Chinese in Manchuria, they declared that no war was being waged, only a bandit extermination drive [2]. In the bombardment of Damascus by the French in 1925 the "distinction between peoples with respect to war" was discussed by jurists [3] and military men [4]. Professor Quincy Wright comments as follows: "Possibly the emphasis, in most accounts

purposes of magic, and the bleeding of infants". *League of nations, Dispute between Ethiopia and Italy, Memorandum by the Italian Government on the Situation in Ethiopia. League of Nations Document*, C. 340. M. 171. 1935. VII. 59.

[1] Cf. *ibid.*, p. 39.

[2] Cf. *Observations of the Japanese Government on the report of the Commission of Enquiry. League of Nations Documents*, C. 775. M. 366. 1932. VII, 32.

[3] Cf. Quincy Wright, "The Bombardment of Damascus", *AJIL*, XX (1926), 263–280.

[4] Cf. Elbridge Colby, "How to Fight Savage Tribes", *AJIL*, XXI (1927), 279–88.

of the recent bombardment of Damascus, upon the fact that relatively slight damage was done to Europeans and Americans indicates the existence of this distinction in the moral sense of western communities" [1]. Captain Elbridge Colby, U.S.A. in a subsequent article in the same journal [2] points out that the distinctioи is made in military practice. Colby writes: "The distinction is existent. It is based on a difference in the methods of waging war and on different doctrines of decency in war" [3].

Although not considering directly the problem of "distinction between peoples with respect to war", Oppenheim covers the matter indirectly in the following words: "The Law of Nations, as a law between States based on the common consent of the members of the Family of Nations, naturally does not contain any rules concerning the intercourse with and treatment of such States as are outside that circle" [4].

A very well known British jurist of the nineteenth century, Lorimer, divided humanity into "three concentric zones or spheres — that of civilized humanity, that of barbarous humanity, and that of savage humanity" [5]. The particular sphere to which a people belonged determined the recognition it received *vis à vis* other states. This notion implies some sort

---

[1] Wright, "Bombardment of Damascus", *op. cit.*, p. 266.

[2] Colby, *op. cit.*

[3] *Ibid.*, p. 273.

[4] L. Oppenheim, *International Law* (3d ed.; London: Longmans, Green and Co., 1920), I, 36.

[5] James Lorimer, *The Institutes of the Law of Nations* (Edinburgh: William Blackwood and Sons, 1883), I, 101.

of "distinction between peoples with respect to war".

It may be pointed out that although there is doubt whether the "distinction between peoples with respect to war" is incorporated in modern international law, nevertheless this distinction does exist in current notions of international morality, and more importantly in contemporary international practice.

The second problem arising in relation to the "legal position of war" is the method of commencing it. Is a "declaration of war" prerequisite? Can there be a war without a declaration? Hall writes that "a declaration in some form is insisted upon by the body of writers" [1]. The Hague Convention (1907) relative to the opening of hostilities reads as follows:

Article Premier

Les Puissances contractantes reconnaissent que les hostilités centre elles ne doivent pas commencer sans un avertisement préalable et non équivoque, qui aura, soit la former d'une déclaration de guerre, soit celle d'un ultimatum avec declaration de guerre conditionelle [2].

This convention might be said to be the current international law on the subject of "declaration of war" as it was ratified by twenty-five leading states including Japan and was generally observed by the states which entered the World War. Seventeen more states including Italy signed the convention, but did not ratify it. In spite of their being signatories to this

---

[1] W. E. Hall, *Treaties on International Law* (6th ed.; Oxford: Clarendon Press, 1909), p. 370.

[2] *Les Conventions de Declarations de la Haye de 1899 et 1907* (New York: Oxford University Press, 1918), p. 96.

convention, both Japan in Manchuria, and Italy in Ethiopia have carried on military aggression without a "declaration of war". Such contemporary situations as these seem to indicate that the question of "declaration of war" is not an academic one but one which has a pertinent bearing on contemporary problems of international relations.

The third problem involved in the study of the "legal position of war" is the "distinction between *just* and *unjust causes* of war". A definition of the "just cause of war" is not opportune in an introduction to a study on the legal position of war because so much of this study will be an inquiry into the various definitions which have been given by different thinkers and writers. It should be pointed out that among some contemporary writers [1] on international law, there has been a tendency to belittle the importance of the "distinctions" between "just and unjust war" and "just and unjust causes of war". This tendency has been indicated in the treatises of these publicists, negatively by the small amount of space given to the statements of such "distinctions", and positively by the arguments made to show the futility of discussing such "distinctions" in a work on international law. They write that such "distinctions" are included under international ethics, and since international ethics are

---

[1] Cf. C. G. Fenwick, *International Law* (1st ed.; New York: Century, 1924), pp. 127–8; A. S. Hershey, *Essentials of Public International Law* (2nd ed.; New York: Macmillan Co., 1927), pp. 533, 552; T. J. Lawrence, *International Law* (4th ed.; Boston: D. C. Heath & Co., 1910), pp. 127–8; L. Oppenheim, *International Law* (4th ed.; London: Longmans, Green and Co., 1928), pp. 127–8.

not part of international law, such "distinctions" do
not belong in a treatise on international law.

The more "philosophical" writers, however, such as
Hans Kelsen [1] and his school, claim that legal norms
determining the just uses of force are the very essence
of all law whether it be municipal or international law.
This "philosophical" school, although priding itself on
its positivism, actually tends to revise some of the
concepts of "natural law", which was regarded formerly as a primary basis of international law, and provided
the "distinction" between just and unjust war.
Professor Kelsen writes: "Whoever denies the theory
of *bellum justum* rejects in truth the legal nature of
international law and assumes a position on which
international law can scarcely claim any validity as a
legal system" [2]. The *bellum justum* theory itself was
implicitly restated in a recent League of Nations report
of the Committee of Six which was adopted by the
Council. The pertinent section of the report reads:
"After an examination of the facts stated above, the
committee has come to the conclusion that the Italian

---

[1] H. Kelsen, *Allgemeine Staatslehre* (Berlin: J. Springer, 1925).

[2] Hans Kelsen, "Rechtstechnik und Abrüstung", *Der Deutsche Volkswirt*, VI (1932), 878:

"Wer die Theorie des *bellum justum* ablehnt, leugnet in Wahr-
heit die Rechtsnatur des Völkerrechts und bezieht eine Position,
von der aus das Völkerrecht kaum überhaupt noch als normative
gelten kann".

Also cf. Eagleton, "The Attempt to Define Aggression", *Inter-
national Conciliation*, Nov. 1930, Number 264 (New York: Carnegie
Endowment). V. H. Rutgers, "La Mise en Harmonie du Pacte de la
Societe des Nations avec le Pacte de Paris", *Hague. Académie de
Droit International. Recueil des Cours* (Paris: Librairie du Recueil
Sirey, 1932), XXXVIII (1931), 5.

Government has resorted to war in disregard of its covenants under Article XII of the League of Nations"[1]. In reference to this report newspapers carried headlines to the effect that "League holds Italy guilty of *unjust war*".

The problem of the "distinction between just and unjust war" is closely associated with the fourth problem to be discussed, "neutrality and the duty of third states to go to war". Various questions are involved in this problem. Can a war be just on both sides? Can only one side have a "just cause"? If these questions are answered in the affirmative, what is the status of third parties? Are they required to go to war against the state waging an "unjust war"?[2] In the past few months there has been much discussion by Senators, publicists, etc. of one aspect of this question, "how should the American neutrality law be stated?" Should the United States follow a policy of "complete" neutrality, or should the United States follow a policy of "partial" neutrality? Some phases of the historical changes in these questions will be treated under "neutrality and the duty of third states to go to war".

The fifth and last problem to be considered in relation to the "legal position of war" is that of "limitation on war with respect to time and place". Time limi-

---

[1] *League of Nations Document* A. 78. 1935. VII, 9. For a recent study of aggression in international law, cf. Quincy Wright, "The Concept of Aggression in International Law", *A JIL*, XXIX (1935), 373–95.

[2] Cf. Quincy Wright, "Collective Rights and Duties for the Enforcement of Treaty Obligations", *Proceedings of the American Society of International Law, 1932*, pp. 101–19.

tations comprise such things as truces and "cooling off" '
periods, the latter being developed in recent times by
the Bryan treaties. The limitations on place as to the
waging of war are exemplified in such modern practices
as the neutralization of Switzerland. Also in the
Covenant of the League of Nations, Article XII, there
is stated a limitation on war with respect to time. It
reads: "The Members of the League agree that, if
there should arise between them any dispute likely
to lead to a rupture, they will submit the matter either
to arbitration or judicial settlement or to inquiry by
the Council and they agree in no case to resort to war
until three months after the award by the arbitrators,
or the judicial decision, or the report by the Council".

In summary, the five problems which will be treated
in this study may be paraphrased into questions. With
whom may a state wage war? How must a state begin
a war? What circumstances justify a war? Under what
conditions is a state obliged to wage war? And when
and where is a state obliged to refrain from waging
war? These problem questions will be investigated by
means of historical evidence. Beginning with ancient
Greece and ending with the eighteenth century, the
characteristic practice and theory in regard to them
will be analyzed. It is not the purpose of this study to
present an exhaustive description and analysis of all
the material relating to the subject for a period of two
thousand years, but to show the characteristic
practice and theory of the main historical periods. The
termination of the investigation with the eighteenth
century has not been made arbitrarily. International

law as it relates to the theory of war took on a new form during the nineteenth century. That century marked an important division in the progress of international law. What followed in the nineteenth and twentieth centuries is of such immense scope that many volumes could be written on that period alone. The present writer hopes that he may some time in the future in a study subsequent to this one, contribute one of the volumes on the recent period. To determine the practice in the different epochs investigated, secondary materials have often been relied upon. The writer has not been able to use all the primary sources relating to war practices from ancient Greece to the French Revolution.

The main part of this study will be an examination of the writings of representative thinkers in the ancient and mediaeval periods, in the Renaissance and Reformation, and in the seventeenth and eighteenth centuries. It is with respect to the "classical" [1] writers on international law of the sixteenth, seventeenth, and eighteenth centuries, that the present writer is especially concerned. Primary sources have been used for this portion of the work.

---

[1] The term "classical" is used here not in reference to ancient Greece and Rome, but as covering the writers beginning with those of the sixteenth century who first wrote on international law as a separate subject.

CHAPTER I

ANCIENT TIMES

Greece

Practice. — The unique system of Greek city-states created a political situation necessary for international law, named a set of relationships between different independent political units. There were treaties at least as far back as the fourteenth century B. C. between the Egyptian Pharaohs and the neighboring kings, but their agreements covered only the relationships between the countries concerned and were not extended to a group of states [1]. The Indian code of Manu of about 500 B. C. was the first written attempt of which records are known to prescribe rules for the conduct of war, but its provisions dealt with only some of the technicalities of practicing warfare [2]. The Hellenic world provides, from what we have record, the first clear example of international law defining relationships between sovereign political units bound together by a common culture and religion.

Although the unit of political organization was the

---

[1] Cf. J. H. Breasted, *Ancient Records of Egypt* (Chicago: University of Chicago Press, 1906), III, 163 ff.

[2] Cf. A. K. Burnell and E. W. Hopkins, *The Ordinances of Manu* (London: Kegan Paul, Trench, Tübner & Co., 1891), Lecture VII.

city-state, there were parts of Greece where this governmental unit was not indigenous. What political organizations existed, however, were of this character[1]. The city-state included all the territory that belonged to the city; consequently its area sometimes reached far beyond the city walls. Each particular city-state had a distinct political consciousness, and considered itself self-governing and self-sufficient, for the state was coextensive with the city. The Greek ideal was preferably perfection within the circle rather than territorial aggrandizement[2]. This did not imply a permanent union of all city-states but the anomalous situation in which people speaking a common language, participating in common sports, worshipping the same goods, and consulting the same oracles were separated into many autonomous communities.

In spite of the political and legal autonomy of the Greek city-states, there was a much greater division between Hellenes and non-Hellenes or barbarians. The latter were regarded by the former as aliens not only in the political and legal sense, but also in the intellectual, moral, and religious sense. It was to the category "beyond the pale of the law" that the non-

---

[1] Cf. E. Barker, *Greek Political Theory* (2d ed.; London: Methuen & Co., 1925); A. Zimmern, *The Greek Commonwealth* (4th ed.; Oxford: Clarendon Press, 1924).

[2] A. E. R. Boak, "Greek Interstate Associations and the League of Nations", *Am. Journal International Law.* XV (1921), 375–383; F. Laurent, *Histoire du Droit des Gens et des Relations Internationales* (Gand: L. Hebbelynck, 1850–70), II, 3; cf. W. S. Ferguson, *Greek Imperialism* (Boston: Houghton Mifflin Co., 1913), pp. 1–35.

Greeks or barbarians were allocated [1]. Consequently
the laws regulating war were not applicable to barbarians [2]. There was, then, in ancient Greece a fairly
clear-cut "distinction between peoples with respect
to war" [3].

With the rise of trade and commerce and the
development of political organization, the character
of war in ancient Greece became more stringently
regulated. Certain practices concerning the commencement of hostilities took on a fairly well defined form.
The most important of these was the declaration of
war with a formal announcement by heralds [4].
Although there were many cases where this practice
was not carried out, they were on the whole quite
exceptional [5]. A well known student of this period,
Coleman Phillipson writes: "Even in the heroic epoch
in Greece no war was undertaken without the belligerents' alleging a definite cause considered by them as a
valid and sufficient justification therefor" [6].

[1] C. Phillipson, *The International Law and Custom of Ancient
Greece and Rome* (London: Macmillian & Co., 1911), I, 40–1.

[2] *Ibid.*, II, 195.

[3] Such a distinction was also held in ancient China. Cf. W. A. P.
Martin, "Traces of International Law in Ancient China", *International Review*, XIV (New York, 1883), 69.

[4] Mauritius Müller–Jochmus, *Geschichte des Völkerrechts im Alterthum* (Leipzig: E. Keil & Comp., 1848), p. 119.

[5] Cf. G. Busolt, *Griechische Staatskunde* (München: Beck, 1926),
II, 1260. "Dieses [Krieg- und Beuterecht] gebot die formliche An-
kündigung des Krieges durch einen Herold (Keryx) vor dem Be-
ginne der Feindseligkeiten. Übertretungen dieser Vorschrift sind
allerdings vorgekommen aber in der Regel hat man sie beobachtet".

[6] Phillipson, *op. cit.*, II, 179. For an interesting example of the
alleging of a definite cause of war, cf. the discussion between the

As to the existence of neutrality in ancient Greece, it can be said that this legal status was manifested in the politics of the time. To be sure, the observer of neutrality was motivated primarily by considerations of national interest rather than of legal obligation, but nevertheless neutrality was often observed by the Hellenic states [1]. It must be pointed out, however, that the strict observance of neutrality in ancient Greece was limited by the custom of establishing confederations and alliances. These sets of relationships were exemplified by such organizations as the first and second Athenian leagues, the Peloponnesian confederacy under the leadership of Sparta, the Achaean league, and the Aetolian league. The objective of these leagues seems to have been to protect the members against any non-members who were potential enemies, or to form an alliance to put down a strong power which was threatening the political welfare of the members of the confederation or alliance. There was the obligation on all the members of the confederations and alliances to help a fellow-member in waging a war with an outside power. The earlier leagues were more lenient than the later ones in allowing their members to wage war on each other. In the later leagues there was the practice of submitting disputes between members to the common assembly which in some cases insisted that its arbitral award be followed. It is impossible, however, to find in any of these leagues a

---

Melians and the Athenians in B. Jowett, trans., *Thucydides* (Oxford: Clarendon Press, 1900), II, 168–9.

[1] *Ibid.*, II, 303.

clearly defined legal relationship requiring all the members to go to war against a recalcitrant member which was attempting to break the peace contrary to the terms of the league.

The limitations on war in ancient Greece in respect to time were confined to a prohibition of warfare during Greek religious festivals and athletic contests and to the existence of treaties of peace, the duration of which was fixed to a certain number of years. It was by means of religious festivals at the shrines of the great gods that there developed a limitation on the time of carrying on hostilities. The celebrated festival of the Olympian Zeus was the outstanding event which made for a temporary peace between all the city-states. This affair participated in by all the Hellenes grew out of the local athletic contests at Olympia, and became an interstate competition under religious auspices. If a city-state did not cease hostilities during the festival, it was punished by exclusion from the games [1]. With reference to time, there was the other form of limitation on war, namely, the existence of treaties of peace. The practice of the city-states was to make with each other treaties of peace which were not intended to be perpetual, but actually were stipulated to cover a definite period of years [2]. The time limits of these treaties were five, ten, thirty, fifty, and even a

---

[1] Cf. Busolt, *op. cit.*, II, 1263.

[2] W. E. Caldwell, *Hellenic Conceptions of Peace* (New York: Columbia University, 1919), p. 44; F. E. Adcock, "Some Aspects of Ancient Greek Diplomacy", *Proceedings of Classical Association of England and Wales*, XXI (1924), 96.

hundred years [1]. During the life of these treaties, city-states were not supposed to make war, but a safe presumption is that many of them did [2].

Closely related to the limitation on war with respect to time was that with respect to place. By international conventions, it was often agreed by Greek city-states to refrain from hostilities in certain places [3]. These places included the important temples and sanctuaries as well as entire cities and large territories. Examples of the latter were the city of Delphi, and the territory of Teos, in Asia Minor. A very characteristic Greek limitation on war with respect to place is evidenced in the oath of the Amphictyonic League [4].

Representative Thinkers. — After this somewhat general background of the status of war in ancient Greece, let us consider the few ideas held by representative Greek thinkers on this subject. An outstanding Greek philosopher whose ideas on war have been preserved is Plato (c. 428–c. 348 B. C.). He regarded war as the natural state of all existence — individual against himself, man against man, family against family, village against village, and country against

---

[1] Busolt, *op. cit.*, p. 1251.

[2] Cf. Sir Paul Vinagradoff, *Outlines of Historical Jurisprudence* (Oxford: Oxford University Press, 1929).

[3] Phillipson, *op. cit.*, II, 301–03; Adcock, *op. cit.*, pp. 105–06.

[4] "We will not destroy any Amphictyonic town nor cut it off from running water, in war or peace. If any one shall do this we will march against him and destroy his city. If any one shall plunder the property of the god, or shall take treacherous counsel against the things in his temple at Delphi, we will punish him with foot and hand and voice, and by every means in our power". Quoted in G. G. Wilson, *International Law* (8th ed.; New York: Silver, Burdett & Co., 1922), p. 16.

country [1]. War, said Plato, is not the result of a primordial condition of man, but is the by-product of civilization. As man learns the art of government, he learns the art of war [2]. It is because man follows expediency and not the good that war occurs [3]. With reference to the distinction between peoples with respect to war, Plato, quite typically of the Greek mind, looked upon all non-Greeks as barbarians and natural enemies on whom perpetual war should be made in the common interest of all Hellenes.

It seems evident that what Plato called war was not war in the sense of modern international law, but competition between individuals and between city-states. Even his own words are proof of this conception; they are: "In reality every city is in a natural state of war with every other, not indeed proclaimed by heralds, but perpetual" [4]. This statement indicates that Plato had two different notions of war, one being competition between city-states, and the other, war in the legal sense. In keeping with this distinction, he regarded organized hostilities between Hellenic city-states not as war, but as "discord and disorder" [5]. Plato applied the term "war" to conflicts between the Greeks on the one hand and the non-Greeks or barbarians on the other.

Plato vaguely implied the notion of a just cause of

---

[1] *Laws* 625 et seq. Cf. Caldwell, *op. cit.*, for reference to the attitudes of Greek thinkers with respect to war.

[2] *Protagoras* 322.

[3] *Laws* 686–89.

[4] *Laws* 626.

[5] *Republic* 470 et seq.

war in saying that war could only be justified by the fact that it was being waged to secure freedom and to achieve a reconciliation. War, said Plato, affords neither instruction nor amusement; peace should be kept as long and as well as it can be [1].

The views of Aristotle (384–322 B. C.) on war resembled very much those of Plato. War is caused by self-interest: men try to exploit the public good for their own gain [2]. It is unlawful for men to dominate over other men for when they do this, they rule without regard to justice [3]. Although it is the business of the leaders of the state to prepare for war, war should be made only for the sake of peace [4]. War is justifiable in three cases: (1) self-defense; [5] (2) to establish a hegemony over those who would thereby be benefited; [6] and (3) to set up a political control over those nations that deserve to be enslaved [7].

Summary. — Although neither the practice nor the thought of ancient Greece developed a clear-cut conception of war as a juridical status, they both contributed something toward the formulation of such a notion. War was not only normal in practice, but also was considered normal by the philosophers. However, most of the kinds of limitation on the making of war, which were worked out more completely in

---

[1] *Laws* 803.
[2] *Politics* IV, 11.
[3] *Ibid.,* VII, 2.
[4] *Rhetoric* I, 4; *Politics* VII, 15.
[5] *Politics* VII, 14.
[6] *Ibid.*
[7] *Ibid.*

subsequent systems of law, were recognized by the
ancient Greeks. War was limited in time and place by
religious customs and by treaties. The requirement of
a formal declaration of war was recognized and often
practiced. Certain thinkers, especially Aristotle, started
the long effort to distinguish just causes of war. Rules
of warfare were observed in wars between Hellenic
states which in this respect were sharply distinguished
from the barbarians, or non-Greeks, against whom
hostilities would be conducted without mercy.

R o m e

Practice. — Though Rome inherited much of Hellenic civilization, her conception of international
relations was somewhat different from that of ancient
Greece [1]. It might be recalled that ancient Greece was
a collection of independent and somewhat equal city-
states; while Rome, on the other hand, through her
superior military and administrative ability established
a dominance over her territories and neighboring
states. It was quite natural that the Romans with this
constant policy of establishing hegemony should call
these communities *hostes*. In spite of the fact that
Rome like Hellas regarded the rules and principles of
war applicable only to sovereign states and not to mere
conglomerations of individuals and in spite of the fact
that she recognized the status of very few political
communities, she did take cognizance of the legal war

---

[1] Baron S. A. Korff, "An Introduction to the History of International Law", *AJIL*, XVIII (1924), 252.

rights of surrounding states. There was in the minds of the Romans, however, the distinction between civilized states on the one hand and barbarian and savage tribes on the other [1]. And of course Rome considered the law of war applicable only to the civilized states [2].

The Roman practice of declaring war was inextricably interwoven with the *jus fetiale* [3]. This law which embraced the procedure for making war was administered by the fetial college. Presiding over this body was the *magister fetialum*. Another important official was the *pater patratus*, who was the delegated

---

[1] The following quotations have been taken from the Digest of Justinian, *Lib.* L. Tit. XVI, 118: "Hostes hisunt, qui nobis, aut quibus nos publice bellum decrevimus exteri latrones, aut praedones sunt". *Lib.* XLIX. Tit. XV, 24: "Hostes sunt, quibus bellum publice Populus Romanus decrevit, vel ipsi Populo Romano: coeteri latrunculi vel praedones appelantur". From *Corpus Juris Civilis*, Ed. Christoph. Henr. Freiesieben, (Coloniae Munatiane, Suptibus E. and J. R. Thurnisiorum Fratum, MDCCXXXV).

[2] Cf. C. Phillipson, *The International Law and Custom of Ancient Greece and Rome* (London: Macmillan & Co., 1911), II, 195–6.

[3] T. Frank, "The Import of the Fetial Institution", *Classical Philology*, VII (1912), 335; and cf. *Roman Imperialism* (New York: Macmillan Co., 1914); D. J. Hill, *A History of Diplomacy in International Development of Europe* (New York: Longmans, Green & Co., 1905), I, 9; Baron Korff, "An Introduction to the History of International Law", *op. cit.*, p. 252; J. A. O. Larsen, "Was Greece Free between 196 and 146 B. C. ?" *Classical Philology*, XXX (1935), 194–7; F. Laurent, *Histoire du Droit des Gens et des Relations Internationales* (Gand: L. Hebbelynck, 1850–70), III, 15–19; C. Phillipson, *op. cit.*, II, 315; T. A. Walker, *A History of the Law of Nations* (Cambridge: University Press 1899), I, 9, 11. Wehberg, *The Outlawry of War* (Washington, D. C.: Carnegie Endowment for International Peace, 1931), p. 1; A. Weiss, "Le Droit Fétial et les Fétiaux à Rome", *La France Judiciaire* (Paris: G. Pedone–Lauriel, 1883).

spokesman of the fetials, when they were sent abroad. The functions of the college were threefold: sacerdotal, diplomatic, and judicial. It is only to the second and third that the practice of declaring war is related. The diplomatic duty of the fetials was to serve as ambassadors, and their judicial function was to decide whether the preliminary proceedings before a contemplated war were conducted in a legal manner.

Whenever Rome had a grievance against some city, a complicated procedure was observed, before she could legally go to war against this political entity. This procedure started with the demand for satisfaction or the *rerum repititio*[1]. This demand was made by the *pater patratus* who was accompanied in his mission by several of his associates in the fetial college [2]. The particular grievance was set forth at the frontiers of the offending city by the *pater patratus*, who then invoked the gods to bear witness to the justice and piety of his demand [3]. After the fetials had duly demanded satisfaction, war could then be legally declared, if the satisfaction was not promptly granted. However, it was held to be wrong and impious to do so, especially if the war had already been resolved upon beforehand, or if the circumstances did not afford the enemy the proper time to make the answer.

Since the sanctioned practice was not to declare war as soon as the demand for satisfaction was tendered to

---

[1] This was known also as *res repetere*, or *repititum ire*, and later was known as *clarigato* or *clarigare*.

[2] Phillipson, *op. cit.*, II, 330.

[3] *Ibid.*, pp. 332–33.

the enemy, the procedure for declaring war did not end at this stage. The fetials returned to Rome, and a period of thirty-three days was allowed to the enemy in order to give satisfaction. If the demand for satisfaction was not given within this period, the *pater patratus* with some fetials was sent again to the defaulting nation to threaten it again with war. After doing this, the *pater patratus* with the fetials appeared before the Senate and informed it that all the ceremonies prescribed by the *jus fetiale* were performed and that war could be legitimately undertaken by Rome to enforce its claim, if the people and the Senate deemed it fit to do so. If the Senate, or the Assembly of the people after the fifth century B. C. voted in favor of war, the *pater patratus* was again dispatched. After he had made solemn pronouncements proclaiming war, he declared war by throwing a javelin on the territory of the enemy. This formal declaration of war was known as the *indictio*.

This elaborate fetial procedure which has just been outlined was not always perfectly observed. In fact, it was dispensed with under certain circumstances. They were as follows: when the enemy was not a body of people organized as a state [1]; when the enemy had made a sudden attack on Rome or its territory; and when there was a civil war.

The fetial procedure became greatly transformed in the last days of the Republic and during the Empire. The prolonged proceedings relating to the proclamation

---

[1] Cf. *supra*, p. 20.

of war were omitted. The javelin was not thrown on the enemy territory, but either on a piece of Roman land which an enemy national would be forced to purchase or at a pillar in a Temple of War representing the enemy territory. Finally, the practice developed of sending images of the javelin to the enemy instead of throwing a real one somewhere. By the fourth century A. D., this most interesting Roman legal institution had entirely disappeared.

With the elaborate procedure of the fetial college there developed the notion of a just war. As has been pointed out, the fetial college determined whether the preliminary proceedings before a contemplated war were conducted in a legal manner. If they were, the war then would be considered just. Due to this practice of getting the preliminaries sanctioned by the fetial college, the Romans regarded every war that they waged as a just one [1]. Some writers [2] on the status of international law in Rome hold that the justness of a war, as decided by the fetial college, covered only the question of whether or not the war was properly declared.

Other writers [3], however, hold that the fetial college

---

[1] Cf. Hill, *op. cit.*, I, 9.

[2] Laurent, *op. cit.*, III, 17; J. Marquardt, *Romische Staatsverwaltung* (Leipzig: S. Hirzel, 1885), III, 427; Phillipson, *op. cit.*, II, 180, and footnote 3 on same page; Baviera, "Il dir. inter. dei Rom.", *Archivio giuridico* (Modena, 1898), Nuova Serie, I and II, 494.

[3] Hill, *op. cit.*, I, 9. T. Frank, "The Import of the Fetial Institution", *Classical Philology*, VII (1912), 335–42: "Of late, to be sure, the general attitude toward the fetial institution has been to hold that its work was not very extensive. Laurent in his influential

not only decided on the justness of a war as measured by its correct declaration but also passed upon the justness of the cause of or grounds for the war. Regardless of whether or not the fetial college inquired into the cause of a war before it pronounced it just, the fact still remains that there were in Rome certain conditions which were considered as just causes of war. They were as follows: violation of a treaty, truce, or armistice; an offense committed against an ally; violation of neutrality; violation of sanctity of ambassadors; refusal to surrender an ambassador who had violated his neutrality; unjustifiable rejection of an embassy; violation of territorial rights; refusal of a peaceful passage of troops; and refusal to surrender an individual who committed a crime [1].

At first, Rome recognized the political independence of regularly organized states [2]. But with the rise of

---

Histoire du droit des gens, III, propounded the theory that the word *justum* was here as in several other legal formulae merely a technical term referring only to the correctness with which the priests performed the necessary formalities at the opening of a war, that in fact any war which had been opened in the prescribed manner was called a *bellum justum*, even though the demands were inequitable. The passage on which he based this claim was Cic. *De rep.* ii 31: 'Our fathers thought no war *justum* unless due request for restitution was first made and the war formally proclaimed'. It is clear that this conclusion rests upon a fallacy of the undistributed middle, furthermore, that it cannot possibly fit in the part of the formula wherein the enemy is charged with having been *injustum* (ego vos testor populum illum injustum esse neque jus persolvere, Livy, *loc. cit.* [i, 32. 7–10]). Yet Laurent's view has constantly gained ground and is now very widely accepted". Müller–Jochmus, *op. cit.*, p. 155. Weiss, *op. cit.*, p. 478.

[1] Cf. Phillipson, *op. cit.*, II, 182 ff.
[2] *Ibid.*, p. 311.

imperial Rome, there developed the customary attitude that those states which were not her allies were her enemies. In fact, no intermediate position was admitted. It was evident that Roman imperialistic policy was by necessity antagonistic to the recognition of neutrality. And moreover, one can see that under this status of political relationships, there was no collective responsibility to preserve the principles of international law. However, "if a state abandoned without just cause and reason an alliance or a confederacy, the other allies or confederates claimed full justification to commence hostilities against the deserter" [1]. Also, "a serious injury wilfully committed against an ally was usually considered as an offense against that ally's confederates, and so a just ground for war on the part of the latter" [2].

In Rome as in ancient Greece, there were instances where the waging of war was limited by time and place. The time limitation is illustrated by the various truces and armistices which were freely granted for different periods of time. It was the purpose of these truces among other things to allow for the necessary time to conduct negotiations and to bury the dead. The extent of these truces was generally for a definite period, one, two, eight, thirty, forty, and even one hundred years. These various truces did not necessarily come into operation at once. They were made effective on a future date or by the happening of certain events. Although it cannot be classified as a truce, that

---

[1] *Ibid.*, p. 183.
[2] *Ibid.*, p. 185.

practice of allowing thirty-three days to elapse between the stating of the demand for satisfaction by the *pater patratus* and the actual beginning of hostilities [1], was nevertheless a very positive time limitation on war.

The place limitation was manifested, as it was in ancient Greece, in the neutralization of temples, sanctuaries, cities, and even territories.

Representative Thinker. — Of the various Roman commentators on the legal position of war, Cicero (106–43 B. C.) was the most outstanding. While other writers such as Virgil, Seneca, Marcus Aurelius, Epictitus, and the Graeco-Roman, Polybius wrote on some of the aspects of war, Cicero seems to have been more representative than any of his contemporaries. Quite characteristic of his time, Cicero saw a distinction between peoples with respect to war. He stated that a collection of human beings did not constitute a people. What made up a people was a group joined together by an agreement covering justice and the preservation of the common good [2]. In various passages, Cicero has given us his ideas on the necessity of declaring war in order that it be just. In one, he stated that in default of a public declaration of war according to the fetial rites, the war should be considered unjust and impious [3]. At another place, he said that no war is

---

[1] Cf. *supra*, p. 23.

[2] *De rep.* i. 25: ".... omnis hominum coetus quoque modo congregatus sed coetus multitudnis iuris consensu et utilitatis commune consociatus".

[3] *De rep.* ii. 17: ".... sanxit fetiali religione ut omne bellum, quod denunciatum indictumque non esset, id iniustum esse atque impium indicaretur".

considered just unless it has been proclaimed and declared, or unless reparation has first been demanded [1]. He reiterated this statement in another passage [2].

When Cicero said that no war was just unless it were properly declared, he is reputed by some scholars to have meant that the formal declaration and announcement of the war was made only after the fetial college had pronounced the war to have a just cause [3]. Cicero, however, has afforded us other comments which prove that he had in mind the concept of a just cause of war. In one, he very clearly makes the assertion that those wars are unjust which are undertaken without cause, and only those wars waged for revenge or defense can be just [4]. Preceding this statement he makes another very cryptic comment in saying that a war is never undertaken by the ideal state except in defense of its honor or its safety [5].

Although there is some possibility that the ideas Cicero had on the doctrine of the just causes of war were partly derived from Aristotle [6], yet the fact remains that there is scarcely any direct relationship

---

[1] *De rep.* iii. 23: ".... nullum bellum iustum habetur nisi denuntiatum nisi indictum, nisi repetitis rebus".

[2] *De officiis* i. 11: "Ac belli quidem aequitas sanctissime fetiali populi Romani iure prescripta est. Ex quo intelligi potest nullum bellum esse iustum nisi quod aut rebus repetitis geratur aut denunciatum ante sit et indictum".

[3] Cf. *supra*, p. 24, footnote 4.

[4] *De rep.* iii. 23: "Illa iniusta bella sunt, quae sunt sine causa suscepta nam extra ulciscendi aut propulsandorum hostium causam bellum geri iustum nullum potest".

[5] *De rep.* iii. 23:

[6] Cf. W. L. Newman, *Politics of Aristotle* (Oxford: Clarendon Press, 1887), I, 328.

between the loosely stated ideas of the Greeks and the succinct and pointed notions of this Roman. The great significance of Cicero for the problems arising under the legal positions of war lies in his very precise definitions of a just war. It was from these definitions that the scholastic writers evolved their notions of just war. To put it briefly, we can say that Cicero had in mind two things when he spoke of a just war, the one that it must be legally declared, and the other that it must have a just cause.

With reference to the idea of neutrality and the duty to go to war, the present writer has found no crystallized statement in the works of Cicero. It might be mentioned in passing that this is no doubt due to the fact that the existence of neutrality in Rome was quite uncertain, and that there was no collective obligation to enforce the principles of international law [1].

As to the attitude of Cicero on the question of the limitations on war with respect to time and place, the works of this great Roman orator afford very little. Indicative of the political thinking of the day, Cicero has left us one passage in which he took cognizance of the practice of making truces with the enemy for a definite period. In this passage [2], he merely commented on the treachery of a general who made a truce for thirty days, but violated it by keeping it only during the day and not the night.

Summary. — The practice and thought of Rome

[1] Cf. *supra*, p. 26.
[2] *De officiis* i. 33:

differed considerably from that of ancient Greece with reference to the juridical status of war. To be sure, there was more equality among states in ancient Greece than in Rome where one state transcended all others. But in spite of this, Rome developed a much more elaborate set of practices concerning war than did ancient Greece. Like the Hellenes, the Romans felt that they were the only people, in the political sense, and therefore only Rome and her neighbors had any privileges that the law of war might afford. The Romans as did the ancient Greeks considered all outsiders as "beyond the pale of the law". The legal practice of declaring war only after a complicated procedure was much more highly developed in Rome than in Greece. With the administration of the *jus fetiale* by the fetial college, there was manifested the idea of the just war, not only just in the required process of its announcement, but also just in the reasons for its causation. In other words, we have in Rome the first clear manifestation of the doctrine of the just cause of war. According to some scholars, the fetial college decided whether a particular set of facts warranted a just cause of war. And moreover, the practice of Rome was to recognize some ten or more political situations which gave a just cause of war. As to the observance of neutrality and to the existence of the idea that there was a duty to go to war when a state broke the peace, it is obvious that these concepts were practically unknown because Rome recognized no political equal, and all states that were not her allies were her enemies. There were in Rome as in

ancient Greece the practices of limiting the time of war
as well as the place of war. However, the Roman
practices were not as well organized as were the Hellenic ones.

The writings of Cicero on the question of war were in
great contrast to those of his Greek predecessors,
Plato and Aristotle. In possession of a legal mind,
Cicero contributed one of the most precise notions
about the juridical status of war than had been worked
out by any writer or jurist up to this time. Quite
typical of the Greek mind, the thought on war in
ancient Greece was philosophical; while also quite
typical of the Roman mind the thought on war in
Rome was legal.

CHAPTER II

THE MIDDLE AGES

Practice. — The form of international relations in mediaeval times varies considerably from that in ancient Greece and Rome. The political persons in the Middle Ages were not independent city-states like ancient Greece, nor one supreme political power like Rome, but a variety of political and religious entities, all competing with each other for something which approached absolute sovereignty. It was the Papacy, the Holy Roman Empire, and a conglomeration of more or less independent feudal kingdoms that eventually made up the intricate system of political units in the historical period that followed the disintegration of the Roman imperial structure.

In the Middle Ages there was an intermittent state of feudal warfare; vassals were waging war upon suzerains, and suzerains upon vassals [1]. Every private dispute, apparently no matter how petty, was preferably settled by some form of private warfare [2]. This

---

[1] J. W. Thompson, *Economic and Social History of the Middle Ages* (New York: Century Co., 1928), p. 666.

[2] For a distinction between public and private warfare in the Middle Ages, cf. G. Butler and S. Maccoby, *The Development of International Law* (London: Longmans, Green & Co., 1928), pp. 4–6. Private war can possibly be defined as war between vassals of the same prince, or between vassals of different princes. Public war is more difficult to define. The question of what constitutes a

created a great disorder within the governing and spiritual forces of Europe. The Church was struggling for political supremacy on the one hand and an augmentation of its spiritual authority on the other. Promiscuous private warfare caused much political confusion; the Empire was decentralized; kingships constituted overlordships; suzerainties were practically powerless. The Church realized that private warfare was a hindrance to its political aspirations. Naturally this endless private warfare resulted in a weakening of the moral influence of the Church, which was the spiritual and moral sovereign over all Christendom. Since these suzerains and vassals were supposedly all Christians, and still at the same time indulging in unceasing private warfare, the Church felt its spiritual and moral authority threatened.

Although the Church promoted the lessening of private warfare [1], it realized that the war spirit was

---

public war is inextricably blended with the problem of sovereignty. The proper authority who may declare war is a most essential factor in the ascertainment of a public war. It was not until the passing of feudalism, and the emergence of the patrimonial state that the question of what made up a public war became settled. Aside from the observance of certain forms for commencing a war, the possession by each of the combatants of the *suprema potestas* inherent in a Commonwealth or *Respublica*, formed perhaps the most important condition precedent to a public war. The question of what constitutes public war is one which is closely related to the whole gamut of theological, legal, and political problems that characterized the middle ages. And it is especially interwoven with the question of sovereignty, its conception, birth, and maturation. (For a discussion of the theory of sovereignty during this period, cf. C. E. Merriam, *History of the Theory of Sovereignty Since Rousseau* [New York: Columbia University Press, 1900], pp. 11–13).

[1] E.g., the Truce and Peace of God. Cf. *infra*, p. 37.

Ballis, War

deeply imbedded in feudal society. This spirit which had formerly manifested itself in only private war was fused by the Church into a crusading zeal. The crusading zeal assumed an almost military and religious fanaticism. It was a holy war of all Christendom against the infidel and consequently everything else was made subservient to it. The petty quarrels and private warfare among the baronage were diverted to some extent into a unified war on Islam [1].

It is fairly obvious that there was in the Middle Ages a distinction between peoples with respect to war. The idea that the Christians were a people quite distinctly separated from the infidels was pretty well fixed in the mediaeval mind. To the Crusades, one must attribute the crystallization of this distinction, for it was that historical event that made the question something more than merely an academic one. The distinction became quite real. When the Crusades were first called by Pope Urban II in 1095 at the Council of Clermont, their justification was partly attributed to the notion that the infidels were by their very nature the enemies of the Christians [2].

It is difficult to say that there was a universally respected practice in the Middle Ages in regard to formal declaration of war. It was the practice, however, to declare war by letter or by the formal

---

[1] Thompson, *op. cit.*, p. 390.
[2] Cf. D. C. Munro, "Speech of Pope Urban II", *American Historical Review*, XI (1906), No. 2, 239; O. J. Thatcher and F. H. McNeal, *Source Book for Mediaeval History* (New York: C. Scribner's Sons, 1905), pp. 518–19.

announcement of a herald [1]. Somewhat resembling the
Roman custom of a thirty-three day period elapsing
between the demand for satisfaction and the commencement of hostilities was the mediaeval French custom
of the "Quarantaine du Roi". This will be discussed in
a later paragraph dealing with the limitation on war
with respect to time [2].

Another notion concerning the legal position of war
that received a great deal of recognition because of the
Crusades was the just cause of war. This notion began
its development in the international relations of Rome.
As has already been pointed out, it was Cicero who
gave this doctrine its most precise formulation in the
Roman period. Throughout the period from the fall
of Rome to the beginning of the Crusades, this doctrine
was being set forth by the early churchmen [3]. The
Crusades gave a new impetus to the actual significance
of this doctrine.

The wars against the infidels gave a new point of
reference to the idea of the just cause of war. In the
opening of the Crusades Pope Urban II must have had
this notion in mind when he remarked: "Fight
righteous wars instead of the iniquitous combats in

---

[1] T. A. Walker, *A History of the Law of Nations* (Cambridge:
University Press, 1899), I, 115; A. Luchaire, *Manuel des Institutions Françaises* (Paris: Hachette et cie., 1892), p. 230.

[2] Cf. *infra*, p. 39.

[3] At the time of the breakdown of the Roman Empire and the
beginning of Christianity, the doctrine of the just cause of war
became well formulated by the patristic writers who wished to
reconcile the Biblical injunctions against fighting and the immediate
problem of defending the Empire against invasion. Cf. *infra*, p. 41.

which you have been engaged" [1]. "Righteous wars"
apparently meant those which had just causes; while
"iniquitous combats" meant those which did not have
just causes. In his speech, the Pope painted a very
lurid picture of the things necessitating the Crusades:
the atrocities committed by the infidels upon the
Christians, the desecration of the holy places, and the
lack of religious enthusiasm in the people [2]. The Pope
as defender of the faith, had justified war on the infidels because they had committed wrongs on the
persons and properties of the Christians.

As to the nature of neutrality in the Middle Ages, it
can be said that the very intricate and personal
character of feudal political relations makes any
exact definition of neutrality impossible. In the
thirteenth century, during the struggle between the
Church and the kings of France and England, a kind
of neutrality existed in the form of the kings getting
the local clergy either to support them or to remain
neutral in their struggle against the papacy [3].

Just as it is difficult to define the kind of neutrality
that existed in the Middle Ages, it is also hard to point
out precisely the nature of a multi-lateral organization
of states that made a state which broke the peace an
ipso facto enemy of all the other states belonging to
the organization. This idea of the duty of third states
to take action in the interest of peace was somewhat

---

[1] Munro, "Speech of Pope Urban II", *loc. cit.*
[2] Thatcher and McNeal, *loc. cit.*
[3] A. C. Krey, "International State of the Middle Ages", *American Historical Review*, XXVIII (1923), 11.

evident in mediaeval times. The papacy from the tenth to the thirteenth centuries constituted an international state [1], which made possible a kind of neutrality as well as a multi-lateral organization for the maintenance of peace.

The most interesting developments which limited the time and place of waging war in the Middle Ages, were the Peace and Truce of God [2]. The former, which regulated the place of waging war and the participants in war, was first proclaimed in the synod of Charroux in southern France in 989, while the latter, which regulated the time of waging war, was first proclaimed in the Council of Elne in Roussillon in 1027. The people were literally sick from warfare, and the Peace of God appeared as a real remedy for their illness. The Church also realized that it would have much to gain from such a movement; not only would its ambition for political supremacy be partially achieved, but also its desire for spiritual and moral control over its wards might be better satisfied. The anarchy resulting from private war would be limited; the political power of the Church would be enhanced; the immorality of

[1] *Ibid.*

[2] Cf. G. Goyau, "L'Église Catholique et le Droit des Gens", *Hague. Académie du Droit International. Recueil des Cours* (Paris: Hachette, 1926), VI (1925), 144; C. H. Hayes, "Truce of God", *Encyclopaedia Brittannica* (14th ed.; New York: Encyclopaedia Britannica Inc., 1929), XXII, 506; Krey, "International State of the Middle Ages", *op. cit.*, pp. 3–4, 6–7; Le Fur, "La Théorie du Droit Naturel depuis le XVIIe Siècle et la Doctrine Moderne", *Hague. Académie du Droit International. Recueil des Cours* (Paris: Hachette, 1928), XVIII (1927), 289; Luchaire, *loc. cit.*; Thompson, *loc. cit.*; Walker, *op. cit.*, pp. 85–86.

vassals and suzerains in waging these wars would be eliminated; and the moral supervision of Christian society would again be carried on by the Church. The Peace of God was manifested by certain prohibitions on the treatment of the property of the Church, the property of the poor, and the peasants themselves. Those who violated the sanctity of these properties and persons were subject to anathema. Feudal lords were made to swear oaths to the effect that they would observe the corporal and property rights of the peasantry. Besides the sanction of excommunication from the Church, "a sort of ecclesiastical 'strike' by which the offices of the Church were stopped until the offender yielded" [1] was utilized in order to bring the recalcitrant barons into the proper military conduct so desired.

The Peace of God did not eliminate private warfare. It proved inadequate partly because it did not have the support of the feudal law, and partly because it did not place any time limit on waging war. The Truce of God was established in order to remedy these insufficiencies of the Peace of God. It found its way into the resolutions and decrees of synods and councils, the proclamations of popes, and the legislation of monarchs. In 1095 Pope Urban II at the Council of Clermont proclaimed it universal law. It provided that on certain days in the week and in certain seasons in the year, private warfare was prohibited. In the twelfth century when the Truce of God was in its most extended form, scarcely one-fourth of the year remained for

---

[1] Thompson, *op. cit.*, p. 669.

fighting [1]. It was an attempt to decrease the amount of warfare by limiting the time in which war could be legally fought.

Another limitation on the time of waging war in the Middle Ages was the practice in France of the "Quarantaine du Roi" [2]. This referred to the practice of a forty-day period elapsing between the outbreak of hostilities begun by the original belligerents and the taking up of arms by the relatives of belligerents. The very personal character of wars in the Middle Ages is indicated by this last condition of the "Quarantaine du Roi". It is very difficult to draw a distinction between public and private warfare in the Middle Ages. Mediaeval thinkers were aware of the difficulty, and they spent considerable time in attempting to define a public war. While they were succeeding in defining, theoretically, public war, the practice of the time was filled with an abundance of examples of the contrary. Until the end of the Middle Ages there were still public wars and private wars. The actual fusion in theory as well as in fact of public war with private war came with the development of the patrimonial state in the sixteenth and seventeenth centuries. Because the notion of sovereignty had been pretty well worked out by this time, the sixteenth and seventeenth centuries saw the fullest development of the idea that a public war existed for the nation as well as for the private

---

[1] Hayes, *loc. cit.*

[2] Cf. Luchaire, *op. cit.*, p. 231; Walker, *loc. cit.* In Germany, the practice was called the "Landfriede", and it operated similarly to the "Quarantaine du Roi", cf. H. Brunner, *Deutsche Rechtsgeschichte* (Leipzig: Von Duncker und Humboldt, 1892), II, 42 ff.

monarch, who was the state. *L'état, c'est moi*! With the breakdown of the patrimonial theory of the state, the doctrine of war for reason of state supplanted the idea of war for the interest of the monarch. Democracy made the interest of the people supercede the interest of the monarch.

Churchmen. — The writers selected because they represented mediaeval thought on the problems which are being considered are Saint Augustine, Isidore of Seville, Saint Thomas Aquinas, Hostiensis, and Lignano. Saint Augustine is the most important early Christian writer. Isidore of Seville is another outstanding writer. Saint Thomas Aquinas is perhaps the greatest doctor of the mediaeval Church. Hostiensis and Lignano are two very well known mediaeval legists. It should be stated, of course, that these five writers do not take in all the mediaeval thought on war. They do, however, deal with practically all the problems arising under the legal position of war during this period. Mention, of course, should be made of Bernard of Clairvaux (1091–1153), John of Salisbury (1115–1180), Boniface (1235–1301), Du Bois (1250–1312), Dante (1265–1321) [1], Marsiglio of Padua (1270–1340) [2], William of Ockam (1280–1347), John of Gerson (1363–

---

[1] We find this writer saying for instance, "but always in quarrels threatening to become matters of war, every effort should be made to settle the dispute through conference, and only as a last resort through battle". Dante *De Monarchia*, Edited and translated by Aurelia Henry (Boston: Houghton, Mifflin and Company, 1904), chap. X, p. 116.

[2] Cf. Otto Gierke, *Political Theories of the Middle Ages*, Trans. by F. W. Maitland (Cambridge: University Press, 1900).

1429), Nicholas of Cues (1431–1449), and Aeneas Sylvius (1405–1464).

What systematic thought there was in the Middle Ages on the question of war, was confined mostly to the problem of the just war. The theory of the just war was worked out by the doctors of the Early Church who were, of course, under the influence of early Christian thought [1]. It was Saint Augustine (354–430) who first developed in mediaeval times a definition of a just war [2]. With the rise of Christianity in the first three centuries, the notion that all war was repugnant to the Christian teaching was fairly

[1] Luigi Sturzo, *The International Community and the Right of War* (New York: Richard R. Smith, Inc., 1930), p. 170. Cf. C. J. Cadoux, *The Early Christian Attitude to War* (London: The Swarthmore Press, Ltd., 1919), pp. 51 ff. Tertullian (155–222) held that Christians should not wage war. There is no record that they did from 50 to 170 A. D.

[2] Cf. A. C. F. Beales, *The History of Peace* (New York: Dial. Press, 1931), p. 19; A. J. Carlyle, *A History of Mediaeval Political Theory in the West* (New York: G. P. Putnam's Sons, 1903), I, 36, 44 ff.; T. E. Holland, *Studies in International Law* (Oxford: Clarendon Press, 1898), pp. 40 ff.; C. L. Lange, *Histoire de l'Internationalisme* (Kristiana: H. Aschenhoug & Co., 1919), pp. 43–4; E. Nys, *Le Droit de la Guerre et les précurseurs de Grotius* (Bruxelles et Leipzig: C. Muquardt, 1882), pp. 25 ff.; E. Nys, *Les Origines du Droit International* (Paris: A. Castaigne, 1894), p. 45; Robert Regout, S. J., *La Doctrine de la Guerre Juste de Saint Augustin à Nos Jours* (Paris: A. Pedone, 1935); Franziskus Stratman, *The Church and War* (New York: P. J. Kenedy and Sons, 1935), pp. 52 ff.; F. E. Tourscher, *War and Peace in Saint Augustine's De Civitate Dei* (Washington: The Catholic Association for International Peace, 1934); A. Vanderpol, *La Doctrine Scolastique du Droit de Guerre* (Paris: A. Pedone, 1925), pp. 50 ff.; H. Wehberg, *The Outlawry of War* (Washington: Carnegie Endowment for International Peace, 1931), p. 2; Yves de la Brière, "La Conception de la Paix et de la Guerre chez Saint Augustin", *Revue de Philosophie*, Nouvelle Serie, Tome I (1930), 557–72.

widespread. The problem of whether or not it was lawful for Christians to bear arms as soldiers of the Empire became a very real one. At first, the attitude was one of disfavor on warfare conducted by Christians but later when the Empire was threatened by the barbarians, there was a great change in thinking [1]. War became justified under certain conditions.

It is in this historical setting that we can consider the contribution of Saint Augustine [2]. He defined a just war as one which has as its end either (1) the avenging of injustices when it is necessary to chastise a city or people which does not punish its subjects for the commission of a bad act, or (2) the restoration of what has unjustly been taken [3]. From this definition, it can be inferred that a just war is one which has a

---

[1] Cf. Sturzo, op. cit., p. 171.

[2] Some scholars differ on the question of whether Saint Ambrose (333–397) or Saint Augustine was the first to develop in mediaeval times the distinction between just and unjust war. In J. E. Ross, *Christian Ethics* (New York: The Devin-Adair Company, 1927), p. 446, there is this statement: "To St. Ambrose we owe the fundamental distinction between a just and an unjust war". In Regout, op. cit., p. 40, there is not the extreme statement as the one just quoted. He writes as follows: "Les conceptions de saint Augustin sur la guerre trouvent donc, à n'en pas doute, un point d'appui dans des écrits antérieurs; toutefois il les a développées avec tant d'ampleur et de logique que, pour la première fois, on peut parler d'une doctrine chrétienne du droit de guerre, bien que réduite à quelques idées fondamentales". The present writer is inclined to believe that such quibbling over priority is beside the main point because it was the Roman, Cicero, who first made the distinction between just and unjust war.

[3] *Quaestionum in Heptateuchen*, Lib. VI, 10: "Justa autem bella definiri solent quae ulciscuntur injurias si qua gens vel civitas quae bello petenda est vel vindicare neglexerit quod a suis improbe factum est, vel reddere quod per injurias ablatum est".

just cause. And a just cause is either the neglect of a city or people to meet out punishment to its citizens who have committed wrongful acts or the unjust theft of properties.

As to the question of the declaration of war, Saint Augustine has left us another significant definition. There were in his time long disputations on who was authorized to make the declaration of war provided, of course, that the war had a just cause. Saint Augustine held that the natural order most favorable to peace among men demands that the decision and power to declare war belongs to the sovereign [1].

Although Saint Augustine does not explicitly state that a just war "must be declared" by the sovereign, the present writer is inclined to believe that the very nature of this patristic writer's definition of the proper declaration of war would imply an inclusion of it in the concept of a just war.

The next important writer who discussed the juridical status of war was Isidore of Seville (c. 570–636). He like his distinguished predecessor, Saint Augustine, did not concern himself with the distinction between peoples with respect to war, neutrality and the duty to go to war, or limitations on war with respect to time and place, but he did define just war. In his substantive distinction between a just and unjust war, he followed the Ciceronian concept as to a just war [2].

---

[1] *Contra Faustum*, Lib. XXII. 75: "Ordo naturalis mortalium paci accomodatus hoc poscit ut suscipiendi belli auctoritas atque consilium penes principes sit".

[2] Nys, *Le Droit de la Guerre*, p. 73. Cf. *supra*, p. 28, n. 2.

Isidore of Seville in his Etymologiae, which appeared about 600, defined a just war as one made, with a declaration, because of things which have been stolen, or because of the enemy's invasion of a state's territory [1]. He defines an unjust war as one made because of fury, and not because of a legitimate reason; he follows up this definition of an unjust war with that of Cicero [2]. It is seen, then, from these definitions that a just war must have, first, a proper declaration, and, second, a just cause, which is the theft of goods or invasion by the enemy. On the other hand, an unjust war is one caused by fury and by no legitimate reason. The present writer has been unable to discover a further elucidation of "de legitima ratione" except that which was given in the definition of a just war. By what Isidore of Seville defined, he attempted to state that war is neither always just nor is it always unjust. The criteria for its justice or injustice depends upon its proper declaration and its just or unjust causation.

Both Saint Augustine and Isidore of Sevilla imply by their definitions of just war that a just cause is

---

[1] Isidori Hispalensis Episcopi, *Etymologiarum sive Originum*, Edited by W. M. Lindsay (Oxford: Clarendon Press, 1911), Lib. XVIII, cap. 1: "Iustum bellum est quod ex praedicto geritur de rebus repetitis aut propulsandorum hostium causa".

[2] *Loc.cit.*, "Iniustum bellum est quod de furore non de legitima ratione initur De quo in Republica Cicero dicit (3, 35): 'Illa iniusta bella sunt quae sunt sine causa suscepta. Nam extra ulciscendi aut propulsandorum hostium causa bellum geri iniustum nullum potest'. Et hoc idem Tullius parvis interiectis subdidit: 'Nullum bellum iustum habetur nisi denuntiatum, nisi dictum, nisi repetitis rebus' ".

necessary in the pursuance of a just war. Each writer states two just causes of war, and of the four just causes given, two of them are the same. Saint Augustine gives neglect of punishment and theft of proper-, ties, and Isidore gives theft of properties and invasion of territory. It is seen that a just cause of war common to both writers is theft of properties, a concept no doubt taken from the civil law. It might be mentioned here that Abelard (1079–1142) reproduces some of these concepts [1].

These definitions found their way into the *Decretum Gratiani* [2]. What it contains pertaining to just and unjust causes of war is mainly a restatement of the concepts of Saint Augustine and Isidore of Seville [3]. It gives three definitions of a just war. The first is that a just war is one that is waged, after a declaration to recover stolen goods or to repel the enemy [4]. The second is that it must be a war which has as its end, (1) either the avenging of injustices when it is necessary to chastise a city or state which does not punish its subjects for the commission of a bad act, (2) or the

---

[1] Cf. Regout, *op. cit.*, p. 48.

[2] Cf. *Cambridge Mediaeval History* (New York: Macmillan Co., 1926), V, 713.

[3] Cf. Vanderpol, *op. cit.*, p. 51.

[4] *Corpus Juris Canonici* (Editio Lipsiensis Secunda post A. E. Richteri, etc.; Leipzig: Tauchnitz, 1879); *Decretum Gratiani.* Causa, XXIII, qu. II, c. 1: "Justum est bellum quod ex edicto geritur de rebus repetendis, aut propulsandorum hostium causa". This definition is that of Isidore of Seville. It was quoted by Ivo of Chartres who made his compilation within less than a century from the *Decretum Gratiani.* Both Gratian and Ivo mention Isidore as inventing this definition. For Ivo, cf. D. Ivonis Carnotensis Episcopi, *Decreti Pars.* X. c. 116; *idem., Panormia,* VIII. c. 54.

restoration of what has unjustly been taken [1]. The third is a war fought because innocent passage of troops has been denied [2]. All this discussion of a just war is preceded by the consideration in the *Decretum Gratiani* of the question of whether or not Christians are prevented from fighting. The *Decretum* holds that they are not [3]. In spite of its mere repetition of the definitions of St. Augustine and Isidore, the *Decretum Gratiani* did contribute something new. It placed them together under their subject matter and therefore was at that time (c. 1140) the most complete "technical treatment of a topic which had hitherto been only considered incidentally" [4].

From the *Decretum Gratiani* the doctrines of just and unjust war passed into the *Summae* of mediaeval churchmen:

"Just as these *Summae* are one of the roots from which sprang the idea of equitable rules superior to the rules of merely human law, so they are one of the chief sources of the rules as to when war may be justly made" [5]. One of the most outstanding of these *Summae* is the *Summa Theologica* of Saint Thomas Aquinas

[1] *Decretum Gratiani*, Causa, XXIII, qu. II, c. 2: "Justa autem bella solent definiri, que ulciscuntur injurias, sic gens et civitas petenda est, que vel vindicare neglexerit quod a suis improbe factum est vel reddere quod per injurias ablatum est". This definition is that of Saint Augustine, cf. *Quaestionum in Heptateuchen*, Lib. VI, 10.
[2] Causa XXIII. qu. II, c. 3.
[3] Causa XXIII. qu. I, c. 1.
[4] T. E. Holland, *Studies in International Law* (Oxford: Clarendon Press, 1898), p. 43.
[5] W. S. Holdsworth, *History of the English Law* (Boston: Little, Brown & Co., 1922–31), V, 30.

(1225–74). In it he states his conception of the criteria of a just war; the first of which is the authority of the prince, the second of which is the just cause, and the third of which is the right intent [1]. The authority of the prince is merely another way of saying that the declaration of war must be made by the legitimate authority [2]. By this definition, then, private warfare is eliminated from the domain of just war because it is not between princes or sovereigns, but between individuals with no supreme political power. The just cause of war was not a new concept at that time,

---

[1] *Summa Theologica*, II. 2. qu. 40, art. 1: "Respondeo dicendum quod ad hoc quod aliquod bellum sit justum, tria requiruntur. Primo quidem auctoritas principis, cujus mandato bellum est gerendum.... Unde Augustinus dicit contra Faustum: 'Ordo naturalis mortalium paci accomodatus hoc poscit, ut suscipiendi belli auctoritas atque consilium penes principes sit'. Secundo requiritur causa justa; ut scilicet illi qui impugnantur, propter aliquam culpam impugnationem mereantur. Unde Augustinus dicit: 'Justa bella solent definiri quae ulciscuntur injurias, si gens, vel civitas plectenda est, quae vel vindicare neglexerit quod a suis improbe factum est, vel reddere quod per injuriam ablatum est'. Tertio requiritur ut sit intentio bellantium recta; qua scilicet intenditur vel ut bonum promoveatur, vel ut malum viteatur. Unde Augustinus: 'Apud veros Dei cultores etiam illa bella pacata sunt, quae non cupiditate, aut crudelitate, sed pacis studio geruntur, ut mali coerceantur, et boni subleventur'. Potest autem contingere ut si sit legitima auctoritas indicentis bellum, et causa justa, nihilominus propter pravam intentionem bellum reddatur illicitum. Dicit enim Augustinus: 'Nocendi cupiditas, ulciscendi crudelitas, impacatus, et implacabilis animus feritas rebellandi, libido dominandi, et si qua sunt similia haec sunt quae in bellis jure culpantur'".

[2] "Accordingly the ascription of a right to wage public war (solemn public war, to use the language of a large majority of writers) was narrowed down to include only the supreme authorities in those Republicae which were distinguished from other Republicae by the acknowledgment of no external domination". Butler and Maccoby, *op. cit.*, pp. 4–5. Also cf. Goebel, *loc. cit.*

but it was the first literal reference to it in the text of any writer. The other writers had not definitely referred to the phrase, "causa justa", but by their contexts they showed that they were inferring such a notion. The just cause given by Saint Thomas Aquinas was nothing more than the one given by Saint Augustine. Saint Thomas Aquinas, however, recognizes this in his text [1]. The just cause was that a wrongful act committed by a people justifies another people in going to war on it, provided that the people committing the wrongful act does not make the amends demanded by the injured people [2]. The right intent was not an original concept of Saint Thomas Aquinas as to defining just war because there is quoted under this point in his *Summa* statements of Saint Augustine to the effect that the true worshippers of God regard as pacific wars those which are not motivated by greed or cruelty, but are intended to punish the wicked and relieve the good from their sufferings [3]. However, one contemporary student of the subject comments on this matter as follows: "Ce passage indiqué par le Décret de Gratien et par Saint Thomas comme extrait des oeuvres de Saint Augustin ne se trouve pas dans les écrits que nous possédons aujourd'hui du grand Docteur" [4]. Saint Thomas Aquinas did not originate this concept because he admits his obligation for it to Saint Augustine. The question is still unsettled, how-

---

[1] He quotes the *Contra Faustum* citation above.
[2] Cf. *supra*, p. 42.
[3] Also cf. *Decretum Gratiani*, Causa, XXIII, qu. 1, c. 6.
[4] Vanderpol, *op. cit.*, footnote, p. 52.

ever, as to whether or not the concept was originated by Saint Augustine. It is seen from these three criteria of a just war, as given by Saint Thomas Aquinas, that they were not new ones, but were drawn from previous writers. These criteria were original only in their arrangement, for none of the previous writers seemed to have included all three of these criteria in their definitions of a just war.

Saint Thomas Aquinas took up an aspect of the question of limiting war with respect to time. In the question of "whether it is lawful to fight on holy days?" he said that while it seems unlawful to fight on holy days, fast days, etc., it is lawful to wage war on these days, provided that it is for the purpose of safeguarding the commonweal [1].

Before ending the discussion of Saint Thomas on war, some mention should be made of the general orientation of this great churchman in the stream of political and moral philosophy. While dividing law into four or five divisions, eternal, divine, natural, human, and international, he regards all law more or less as a set of moral principles.

Legists. — The representative thinkers so far discussed in this chapter were all churchmen. All of them were primarily concerned in discussing a just war from the point of view of its "moral and inward bearings" [2], while the legists, exemplified by Hostiensis and Lignano, who are the two other representative mediaeval thinkers presented in this chapter, were

---

[1] *Summa*, II, qu. 40, art. 4.

[2] Sturzo, *op. cit.*, p. 177.

primarily interested in analyzing a just war from the standpoint of its "authority and organization" [1]. The legists attempted to specify and classify wars as just or unjust according to certain fixed categories. Hostiensis (1210–71) not only defined a just war as having (1) the necessary authority, (2) a just cause, and (3) the right intent as did his illustrious contemporary, Saint Thomas Aquinas [2], but also did something more. He attempted to classify wars by distinguishing seven kinds of war, four of which were just and three of which were unjust [3]. In his *Aurea Summa*, he listed the just wars as: (1) "bellum romanum", which is waged by believers against infidels, (2) "bellum judicale", which is waged by those believers who have the authority of a judge, (3) "bellum licitum", which is waged on the authority of a prince, and (4) "bellum necessarium", which is waged by believers in self-defense. And he classified the unjust wars as: (1) "bellum praesumptuosum", which is waged by rebels in contempt of authority, (2) "bellum temerarium", which is waged by believers against legal authority, and (3) "bellum voluntarium", which is waged by believers on their own authority. It is apparent that this classification of wars into just and unjust merely dealt with the authorization of and participation in war. Hostiensis was primarily concerned with the distinction between peoples with respect to war, and

---

[1] *Ibid.*

[2] Vanderpol, *op. cit.*, p. 56.

Cf. Lange, *op. cit.*, p. 44; Nys, *Les Origines du Droit International*, p. 102.

the declaration of war, and secondarily interested in the just cause of war.

Johannis de Lignano (d. 1383) [1] carried on some of the doctrines of Hostiensis, and climaxed them with a justification of the temporal supremacy of the papacy. His chief work, *De Bello, De Represalis, et De Duello* [2], which appeared in 1360, was another attempt to justify particular kinds of war. War is defined as "a contention arising by reason of something discordant offered to human desire; tending to exclude the discordancy" [3]. Under this definition practically anything can be included as a cause of war because "human desire" encompasses almost anything, and a "discordancy" to it would be the opposite of the "desire"; therefore anything can be a cause of the "discordancy" which is in turn the cause of war. Since war tends to exclude the discordancy, and since the object of all strife is the reassurance of peace, then war is made for the sake of peace. The lawfullness of war is established, according to Lignano, by the Digest of Justinian, and the writings of Saint Augustine.

A very unique and novel classification of the kinds of war is given by Lignano. There are two main kinds of war, "spiritual war", and "corporeal war"; the

---

[1] Was Professor of Civil and Canon Law at the University of Bologna from 1351 to 1383, and during this time was legal adviser to the papacy. Cf. "Introduction" by T. E. Holland in *De Bello, De Represalis, et De Duello* (Oxford: Carnegie Institution, 1917), for a biographical sketch of Lignano.

[2] Johannis de Lignano, *De Bello, De Represalis, et De Duello*, Edited by T. E. Holland, and English translation by J. L. Brierly (Oxford: Carnegie Institution, 1917).

[3] Lignano, *op. cit.*, p. 216.

former is divided into two classes, "celestial" and "human", and the latter is also divided into two classes, "universal" and "particular".

"Celestial spiritual war" is, as the name implies, a war between the spirits of the heavens. Its origin goes back to the time when Lucifer was waging war with the other angels in the heavens; [1] he was not victorious, and consequently was banished from the celestial world. This conflict, which was the first "war", resulted in the victory of Virtue, the Most High, over Vice, the Devil, and demonstrated once and for all that Virtue will remain victorious; provided that it will always put up a real fight with the Devil. In addition to this strife between Virtue and Vice in the heavens, there is the struggle between the celestial bodies themselves. Nature provides that some of the celestial bodies will be in harmony with each other; while others will be in discord with each other. It is in the very nature of things that the universe is not in perfect harmony.

"Human spiritual war" is caused by two things: the first of which is the conflict between Virtue and Vice in every individual, and the second of which is the conflict between reason and appetite in every individual [2]. The first cause, the conflict between Virtue and Vice, was brought to man by Lucifer who was controlled by the Devil, and has been breathed into the

[1] Lignano, *op. cit.*, p. 218: "Arose because of ingratitude arising from a defect in the impress of charity stamped by the Creator on an intelligence, the most sublime of all created intelligences".

[2] *Ibid.*, p. 222.

soul of every man; consequently man must always be battling with sin. In order to substantiate this doctrine, Lignano quotes the following biblical passage: [1] "'Take unto you the armour of God so that ye may be able to withstand the deceits of the Devil'. Ephesians 6 : 11". The second cause, the conflict between reason and appetite, is a variation of the first cause, and is also found in the very nature of things. Passion struggles with intellect, and so the individual is the center of this kind of "war".

"Universal corporeal war" is war between states, and approaches most nearly of all of Lignano's kinds and classes of war to the modern definition of war. However, its causes are exceedingly different from what present publicists regard as the causes of war. In the language of Lignano, this phenomenon of "universal corporeal war" occurs by "virtual opposition of the motions and aspects of celestial bodies, which introduces formal opposition in these lower bodies. . . . whereby the lower wars are introduced" [2]. States similarly to celestial bodies do not stand still and do not remain in a peaceful status because naturally states, like celestial bodies, have an affinity for or an antipathy to each other. Conflicting celestial bodies influence states to conflict with each other. Conflicting states cause loves and hates, and loves and hates give rise to wars. By these interesting analogies, Lignano attempts to show that wars are caused by events which have been happening in the universe of which the world is an important part.

---

[1] *Ibid.*   [2] *Ibid.*, p. 219.

The justification for wars between states is almost as interesting as their origin. Wars are justified by both Divine Law, and the Law of Nations. In dealing with the first reason, Lignano states that "wars were introduced not only with the permission, but by the positive allowance of the Lord" [1]. This statement he attempts to prove by the following syllogism [2]. "Every power tending to good is so derived positively (from God), and not merely permissively" [3]. This is established by the first chapter of the Book of James. "But the power of declaring lawful war tends to good" [4]. This is taken on authority of Saint Augustine. "Therefore it [the power of declaring lawful war] proceeds positively from God" [5]. As to the logical validity of such a syllogism and the two authorities for the major and minor premises, the present writer will not comment, but he wishes to note here that although the syllogism, per se, might not mean very much, it, at least, is indicative of the importance of a problem which was confronting Lignano. This problem was the justification of war by Divine Law.

In dealing with the second reason for the justification of war, Lignano states that the Law of Nations is the same as the Law of Nature [6]. And if war is to be justified by the Law of Nations, it really is justified by the Law of Nature. The Law of Nature emanates from the natural order of things in which there are certain general principles. One of these is that every "natural entity" is vested with the "natural incli-

---

[1] *Ibid.*, p. 224.   [2] *Ibid.*   [3] *Ibid.*
[4] *Ibid.*   [5] *Ibid.*   [6] *Ibid.*, p. 229.

nation to exclude everything opposed to its natural disposition" [1]. This is illustrated with the case of fire and water [2]; fire has a natural antipathy to water, and vice versa. Since states are also "natural entities", they have natural antipathies to other states. From these natural antipathies wars have evolved.

Due to the fact that "the power of declaring lawful war proceeds positively from God" [3], it can be inferred, since the papacy is God's highest agent on the earth, that "the power of declaring lawful war" proceeds from the papacy. Although there is a duality in the world between temporal and spiritual authority, yet in case of conflict, the papacy is always supreme [4]. War may be declared by the Emperor, but only when the Emperor is acting under the authority of the Pope. All Christian sovereigns are agents of the papacy; hence as agents they must carry out the orders of the principal. The Emperor can never rightfully declare war on the Pope, and if he does, he will not have the support of his vassals, for these persons have a prior loyalty, which is to the Pope [5]. It is seen from this that in the last analysis the war making power is solely held by the papacy. And a general rule may be laid down to the effect that one of the requisites to a lawful or just war is its authorization in fact or in name by the papacy.

As to the justification of war on particular kinds of

---

[1] *Ibid.*, p. 230.   [2] *Ibid.*   [3] Cf. *supra*, p. 54.
[4] Lignano, *op. cit.*, p. 231.
[5] *Ibid.*, p. 235: "All the faithful are bound to help the Pope and even the vassals of the Emperor may be absolved from the oath which binds them or may be declared to be bound".

people, Lignano presents some interesting statements. The Pope, as trustee of the world, has jurisdiction over all of the inhabitants therein, regardless of whether or not they are Jews, infidels, or Christians. This gives the Pope the right to punish Jews and infidels for not living according to the Law of Nature, and Christians for not abiding by the Law of the Gospel in addition to the Law of Nature [1]. The Pope directly through himself, or indirectly through the Emperor can declare war legally against practically anyone. Since the Emperor is the agent of the Pope, anyone who resists the authority of the Emperor also resists the authority of the Pope [2]. This is a gross violation of all law; consequently the violator can be legally punished by means of war. The violation is, in our terminology, a just cause of war.

"Particular corporeal war" is Lignano's fourth and last class of war. It is that form of combat which is marked by the self-defense of one person or a group of persons [3]. In the first instance, the self-defense con-

---

[1] *Ibid.*, p. 232.

[2] *Ibid.*, p. 233: "And herein war claims its place, and therefore it is declared by the Roman people or Emperor, so that if the Emperor declares war on any rebellious cities of Italy, that war ranks as a public war because to resist an official of the Emperor or of the Pope, if the resistance is not in the name of the Emperor or the Pope, is one and the same thing".
The justification of declaration of war on the rebellious Italian cities is one of the main purposes of Lignano in writing *De Bello, De Represalis, et De Duello* because he wished to justify the actions of Cardinal Albornoz, the famous warlike papal legate, who was at the time of the writing of the book, waging war in the name of the Pope on the rebellious Italian cities, of which Bologna, the city of Lignano, was a leading one.

[3] *Ibid.*, p. 277.

stitutes a duel, and in the second instance, it constitutes a defensive war; both of them are legal because they proceed from "natural law, and not positive law, civil or canon" [1].

Lignano seemingly makes no reconciliation between "universal corporeal war" justified by divine law and "particular corporeal war" justified by natural law. He appears to hold that divine law legalizes the action of the Pope in waging war upon states which violate his authority. On the other hand natural law would legalize the resistance of those states to the Papacy, although this conclusion is not specifically stated.

Lignano repeats Hostiensis' seven-fold classification of corporeal wars, four of them being just and three, unjust [2]. As these have been discussed in preceding pages [3], the present writer sees no need in restating them.

In summarizing his treatment of the question of the legality of war, Lignano states as follows: ".... wars are said to be lawful by reason of the person declaring them, the person against whom they are declared, the thing, and the cause, and the law which allows them" [4]. On this statement, he cites Saint Thomas Aquinas [5], and Hostiensis [6]. It has been pointed out that Lignano means by "reason of the person declaring them", a war which is declared by the Pope, or his agent, the Emperor. By "the person against whom they are declared", he means the Jews, the infidels, rebelli-

[1] *Ibid.*, p. 278.　　[2] *Ibid.*, p. 276.
[3] Cf. *supra*, p. 50.
[4] Lignano, *op. cit.*, p. 276.
[5] Cf. *supra*, p. 47.
[6] Cf. *supra*, p. 50.

ous Italian cities, and anyone else who resists the authority of the papacy. By "the cause", he means the recalcitrance of a people who have committed a wrongful act, to make the proper amends demanded by the injured people [1]. And by "the law", he means the Divine Law and the Law of Nature. It is interesting to note that the just cause of war, which Lignano gives, is very similar to that concept given by Saint Augustine [2] and repeated by Saint Thomas Aquinas [3]. In so far as an original concept of a just cause of war is concerned, Lignano contributes nothing. He does, however, give us a very novel and unique justification for war by his clever definitions, and most entertaining classifications. But all of his arguments concentrate themselves into the single purpose of proving the supremacy of the papacy in all matters, temporal as well as spiritual.

Summary. — The juridical status of war in the Middle Ages differed greatly from that in ancient Greece and Rome. The practice of waging war at the dawn of the Middle Ages was directed to strengthening the Roman Empire, on the one hand, and maintaining the supremacy of the papacy, on the other, while the thinking on the question of justifying war, which followed because the of practice, was a counter-action against the current Christian viewpoint that war was against the teachings of Christ. The Empire was

---

[1] Lignano, *op. cit.*, p. 276: "But generally there is one justifying cause, the contumacy of one who resists unlawfully. For when justice cannot be had from one who is liable, then war may be declared, for recourse is had to that instrument for help".

[2] Cf. *supra*, p. 42.   [3] Cf. *supra*, pp. 47-8.

contending with various barbarian communities, for its very life. One of the internal obstacles which prevented the Roman Empire from keeping its possessions was this Christian attitude that participation in war constituted a breach of faith. The problem, then, was to find a justification for Christians waging war. Here, we find the contributions of the churchmen. They were primarily concerned with rationalizing the justice of war by laying down certain qualifying categories on the intrinsic character of the war. These writers like Saint Augustine, Isidore of Seville, and Saint Thomas Aquinas held that a just war was one made on declaration of legitimate authority, with a just cause, and for the right intent. The definitions of a just war which these churchmen worked out were obviously based on the Ciceronian concept of a just war [1]. Saint Thomas Aquinas gave perhaps the most complete definition, but as has been pointed out [2], his definition was based on that of Saint Augustine.

With the countless private wars that cursed the early Middle Ages, there arose the problem of putting some stop to them; so that the Church could broaden its authority and so that the Holy Roman Empire could be made sovereign. The institutions of the Truce and Peace of God and of the "Quarantaine du Roi", limitations on the time and place of war, were made in order to tone down the warlike spirit of the mediaeval peoples and had a measure of success at a time when people had suffered severely from the ravages of private war. The Crusades, which began in 1095, open-

[1] Cf. *supra*, p. 28.   [2] Cf. *supra*, pp. 48–9.

ed up new questions for the scholastic writers. Besides
the perennial question of the intrinsic justice of the
Crusades as to their having a just cause, there was the
matter of distinguishing them from other kinds of war
because of the nature of the people with whom they
were fought. Here we have the contributions of the
legists like Hostiensis and Lignano who were primarily
concerned with the distinction between peoples with
respect to war, and the declaration of war. These legists
sought to classify wars as to just or unjust, according
to their authority, i.e., by whom declared, and to their
kind, i.e., between whom fought. The problem of the
declaration of war was almost an endemic one especially in the later Middle Ages not only because of the
question of the sovereignty of the Emperor over his
political subordinates, but also because of the dispute
between the Church and the State as to who had the
final word in political matters, of which the right of
declaring war was a foremost one.

It can be seen, then, that the Middle Ages contributed a great deal to the practice and thought of the
juridical status of war. The distinction between peoples
with respect to war, the declaration of war, the just
cause of war, and the limitations on war with respect
to time and place were all manifested in the practice
and thought of the mediaeval period. Probably the
greatest contribution of the Middle Ages to the subject
of the juridical status of war was the very neat set of
definitions of a just war that were worked out by the
mediaeval churchmen and legists.

CHAPTER III

RENAISSANCE AND REFORMATION

Practice. — The trend of scholastic thought was diverted during the Renaissance. This period ushered in the beginning of what may be called modern history. During the later Middle Ages, whatever existed in the form of European unity was destroyed with the collapse of the Empire and the decay of the papacy. States became governed by monarchs who were absolute in both theory and practice. Besides having political power, the monarchs had enormous military strength in their standing armies. This institution of a permanent professional army became increasingly prevalent among the European states.

Concurrent with this development, the system of balance of power appeared. In Italy the petty states found security in this system. Soon the states of central and western Europe took over this institution which they used as a susbtitute for the system of Empire and papacy. To a certain extent the papacy had been the guardian of international morality and the Emperor had been a means of solidifying the unity of states. The mediaeval political system, however, was destroyed by the decay of feudalism. The states of Europe were thrown into a condition of international anarchy, which was synchronized with the rise of modern nationalism [1].

Towards the end of the fifteenth century explorations were made which resulted in the discoveries in the New World. The treatment of the Indians by the Spaniards, Cortez in Mexico, and Pizarro in Peru, and innumerable lesser combats in Latin America raised the objections of such men as Bartholomew de Las Casas. The Humanistic movement which was sweeping over Europe at about this time was questioning the existing customs. The practice of the Spanish *conquistadores* in conquering the Indians in the New World was to treat them as barbarians outside of the influence of the laws of war which were recognized at that time by the states of Europe [2]. This was also the practice of the Europeans in their treatment of the Turks.

The question of who might declare war was directly related to the waning of the power of the Emperor and of the Pope. The Pope was devoid of any direct political control over the sovereign states of Europe and likewise the Emperor was powerless when it came to an absolute direction of the affairs of these states. It was the sovereign, the absolute monarch, who possessed exclusively the right of war [3]. Such sovereigns as Francis I of France and Charles V of Spain and many other kings and rulers of the states of

---

[1] Cf. R. B. Mowat, *A History of European Diplomacy, 1451–1789* (London: Edwin Arnold & Co., 1928), pp. 3, 4.

[2] Cf. Butler and Maccoby, *op. cit.*, p. 20.

[3] Sturzo, *op. cit.*, p. 180.

Europe had the independent and absolute power to declare war. In the fifteenth and sixteenth centuries there were still instances of declaring war by means of a herald.

> In the middle of the fifteenth century, Edward IV declared war against Louis XI in a letter of fine language and style, carried by Garter, King of Arms. Louis dismissed the Herald with a present of three hundred crowns and thirty yards of velvet. In 1557 Queen Mary (Holingshead tells us) sent a defiance by Clarencieux to Henry II of France. This was, it would seem, the last instance, on the part of England of defiance by Herald. But the custom lasted longer on the Continent [1].

Just as the problem of the declaration of war was dependent on the passing of feudalism so also were the old concepts of the just war and the just cause of war directly related to the new political structure. Scholastic thought continued but not in the old environment of the Middle Ages. It existed in the new background — the European state system. "The meaning of the theory of the Just War had moved to new horizons" [2].

With the passing of the Middle Ages the practice of neutrality was made a little more possible. States were becoming more independent and were beginning to enjoy a right of non-interference from their neighbors. With the rise of the balance of power idea, the old notion that every state was obligated to discriminate between the just and unjust belligerent, disappeared.

---

[1] T. E. Holland, *Lectures on International Law* (London: Sweet and Maxwell Ltd., 1933), p. 252.
[2] Sturzo, *op. cit.*, p. 180.

States recognized a condition of abstention from hostilities, whether these were deemed justly or unjustly undertaken, as a possible position for other states to adopt in such cases as were covered by the signature of an *abstentia guerrarum* on their part with other contractors. Such contracts as the treaty of 1463 between Scotland and Denmark may be cited as containing instances of the *abstentia guerrarum* [1].

It is also worth noting that the Hanseatic towns maintained neutrality when Queen Elizabeth took contraband measures against Spain [2].

The system of the balance of power almost predicates a network of defensive alliances. The Italian city-states of Milan, Naples, Venice, and Florence divided among themselves the Italian peninsula so that no one state could dominate the whole. Thus by nicely adjusting the balance of power in Italy, they maintained a partial independence in the fourteenth century [3]. In 1454 by the "Peace of Lodi" the Italian city-states combined into an alliance to prevent France from coming into Italy. Similar alliances of which other European states were parties were the League of Venice (1495) and the League of Cambrai (1508). In 1518 a treaty was signed which enunciated the principle of universal peace.

The signatory powers mutually guaranteed each other's possessions; other powers were to be invited to adhere to the peace, which would be under the guarantee of the principle contracting parties (*principaliter contrahentes confoederati*). All the numerous allies of the contracting parties were stated to be comprehended within the league [4].

[1] Butler and Maccoby, *op. cit.*, p. 231.
[2] *Ibid.*, p. 25.
[3] Mowat, *op. cit.*, p. 28.
[4] *Ibid.*, p. 42.

This peace was upset by England. It can be seen that there was a crude beginning of a kind of multilateral treaty which obligated the signatories to keep peace among themselves, and if one of them broke the peace against any other, to allow the remaining states of the treaty to go to war against the recalcitrant state. This was the nature of the alliances of the Italian city-states. Their treaties were not designed to prevent war, per se, but were made to preserve the balance of power. Scarcely any permanence was established by these agreements. They would last only three or four years. Two prominent British students of the history of international law have made an interesting comment on the duty of third states to go to war.

> One anomalous feature can be observed throughout the more than one thousand years of Christian discussion of just and unjust war. No duty is enjoined upon princes who are not parties to the dispute to intervene in aid of the just belligerent or even to protect him from the worst consequences of an unfortunate battle [1].

Closely associated with neutrality was a kind of limitation on the place of waging war. During this period there was a practice of a belligerent conceding to a particular area immunity from attack. An illustration of this is the case where the bishopric of Cambrai the county and town of Cambrino were given letters of neutrality by Francis I in 1542 [2]. It is difficult to find in this period any limitation on war with respect to time. The international anarchy of the

---

[1] Butler and Maccoby, *op. cit.*, p. 115.

[2] E. Nys, *Le Droit International* (Bruxelles: A. Castaigne, 1906), III, 536.

day prevented any widely practiced means of limiting war.

Renaissance Humanists and Reformers. — The Renaissance and Reformation introduced a new trend of thought on all problems concerning man. This is apparent in the discussions on war. Writers turned away from the mediaeval ways of thinking which were manifested in quoting Aristotle and in relying on the churchmen. There was a tendency to look at the intrinsic nature of every human problem. We find this innovation in the writings of the Renaissance humanists and reformers. For the representative thinking on the question of war, a selection has been made on the basis of the outstanding men and nationalities of the period. The ideas of the writers to be presented are those of Machiavelli, an Italian, Luther, a German, Erasmus, a Dutchman, and More and Bacon, Englishmen. This is not, of course, a complete list. Other names which might be included are those of Leonardo (1452–1519), Savonarola (1452–1498), Rabelais (1495–1553), Calvin (1509–64), Bodin (1530–96) [2], Montaigne (1533–92), Cervantes (1547–1616), and Campanella (1568–1639).

Into the environment of the international chaos of the fifteenth and sixteenth centuries came Machiavelli

---

[1] It is interesting to note that Bodin was very similar to Machiavelli (cf. *infra*, pp. 59–60), in his conception of the just war. A just war to both Bodin and Machiavelli is a war which is necessary. Cf. A. Gardot, "Jean Bodin, sa place parmi les fondateurs du droit international", *Hague. Académie de Droit International. Recueil des Cours* (Paris: Librairie du Recueil Sirey, 1935), L (1934), 67ε.

(1469–1527) [1]. This renowned political commentator took a very active part in Italian politics. His keen observations on the working of the Italian city-states are famous. Machiavelli, aside from his own political advancement, was very much interested in the realization of the political unity and prosperity of the Italian city-states. Thoroughly imbued with the spirit of the Renaissance, his approach to the problem of war was quite new. Since ancient times, the principal writers on war had been churchmen and legists who followed the methods and dogmas of scholasticism. Machiavelli held in scorn this approach. The method of Machiavelli was the use of history. He believed that the proper approach to an understanding of politics was a study of how politics were practiced in the past. This attitude brought him to a separation of politics from ethics, and furthermore a distinction between public and private morality.

One would expect to find in Machiavelli, and one

---

[1] *The Historical, Political, and Diplomatic Writings of Niccolo Machiavelli*, Trans. by C. E. Detmold (Boston: James Osgood & Co., 1882). For background material, cf. J. W. Allen, *A History of Political Thought in the Sixteenth Century* (New York: The Dial Press, 1928), pp. 447–94; W. A. Dunning, *A History of Political Theories; Ancient and Mediaeval* (New York: Macmillan Co., 1923), pp. 285–327; Louis Dyer, *Machiavelli and the Modern State* (Boston: Ginn & Co., 1904); G. Engelman, *Political Philosophy* (New York: Harper's 1927), pp. 114–34; R. G. Gettell, *History of Political Thought* (New York: Century, 1924), pp. 138–42; F. J. C. Hearnshaw, *Social and Political Ideas of Some of the Great Thinkers of the Renaissance and the Reformation* (London: George C. Harrop & Co., 1925), pp. 87–121; F. Meinecke, *Die Idee der Staatsräson* (München und Berlin: Druck und Verlag von R. Oldernbourg, 1924), pp. 31–60; J. A. Symonds, *Renaissance in Italy* (New York: Henry Holt & Co., 1887).

does, the absence of any careful analysis of the legality
of war. His *Prince* is a manual showing the means to
preserve the State, and his *Art of War* is a statement
of military strategy. In his *Thoughts of a Statesman*,
Chapter II, "Peace and War" [1], he writes as follows:

> That war is just which is necessary. The people will
> complain of a war made without reason. Not he who first
> takes to arms is the cause of the mischief, but he who gives
> the first cause for taking arms.

This passage is about the most definite statement
that the distinguished Italian has given us on this
subject. In his proposition "that war is just which is
necessary", he sets up quite a new doctrine, namely,
that the justness of a war is determined by its necessity. The mediaeval churchmen and legists, in contradistinction to Machiavelli, had stated much earlier
that a war was just when it had a just cause and was
necessary [2]. Justice and necessity did not mean the
same thing to the schoolmen of the Middle Ages as
they did to Machiavelli. The necessity of a war was
only one of the conditions of its justice, according to
the schoolmen; while with Machiavelli, the elements of
justice of a particular war were included in the element
of necessity of the war. The quotations, "The people
will complain of a war made without reason" and "not
he who first takes to arms is the cause of the mischief,
but he who gives the first cause for taking arms" seem
to imply the notion that the necessity of a war is
determined by the reason of state or the utility of the

---

[1] *Writings of Machiavelli*, II, 439.
[2] Cf. *supra*, pp. 40 ff.

war. Is it useful for the state to fight a particular war? Of course it should be noted that although the people demand a reason or a just cause of war, from the sovereign there is only one ultimate equivalent for justice; that is utility. Here is the central point of Machiavelli's thought on this problem. The utility of a war was decided by the sovereign who, of course, had the sole power of declaring war, according to Machiavelli. Such a doctrine, that war is just when it is for the reason of state, was qiute natural for the age of the despots among whom Machiavelli worked and lived.

During the lifetime of Machiavelli there lived in Germany a man who had as much eftect on his country and on the course of world history as did Machiavelli on Italy and the development of state-craft. This was Martin Luther (1483–1546)[1]. The significance of Luther and his followers is that they destroyed the unity of the Church, drove Europe into two armed camps and disdained all authority and tradition[2]. It is impossible to separate Luther's politics from his theology. In his tract *Ob Kriegsleute auch in seligem lande sein können* (Whether soldiers,

[1] Cf. Allen, *op. cit.*, pp. 15–34; W. A. Dunning, *A History of Political Theories, from Luther to Montesquieu* (New York: Macmillan & Co., 1927), pp. 1–14. Gettell, *op. cit.*, pp. 149–151; Hearnshaw, *op. cit.*, pp. 171–91; Preserved Smith, *Age of the Reformation* (New York: Macmillan & Co., 1920); P. Smith, *Life and Letters of Martin Luther* (Boston: Houghton Mifflin, 1911); L. H. Waring, *Political Theories of Martin Luther* (New York: G. P. Putnam's Sons, 1910), I, 8.

[2] Preserved Smith, *A History of Modern Culture* (New York: Macmillan, 1930).

too, can be saved), 1526, Luther delivers a polemic
for certain kinds of war [1]. It is worth pointing out here
that Luther was attempting to justify the active
resistance of the Protestant princes to the Catholic
princes. He tries to do this by distinguishing three
kinds of war.

> First, Wars may be made by three kinds of people. An
> equal may make war against his equal, that is, of the two
> persons neither is the vassal or the subject of the other,
> though the one may be less great or glorious or mighty
> than the other. Or a superior may fight against his inferior.
> Or an inferior may fight against his superior [2].

Luther justifies the war of equals against equals.

> Therefore our conclusion on this point is that war against
> equals should be a thing that is made necessary and should
> be fought in the fear of God. It is made necessary when
> an enemy or neighbor makes the attack and starts the
> war and will not help when one offers to settle the case by
> legal procedure, discussion, or agreement [3].

As for the war of superiors against inferiors he says
this is a right inherent in the nature of political
relationships.

> We have indeed heard above that subjects are to be
> obedient and are even to suffer wrong from their tyrants,
> so that, if things go well the rulers will have nothing to do
> with their subjects except cultivate right, righteousness
> and judgment, but if they rise and rebel, as the peasants
> did lately then it is right and proper to fight against them.
> That too is what a prince should do to his nobles, an
> emperor to his princes, if they are rebellious and start a
> war [4].

---

[1] Martin Luther, *Works*, trans. by C. M. Jacobs (Philadelphia:
A. J. Holman, 1931).
[2] *Works*, V, 42–43.
[3] *Ibid.*, p. 62.   [4] *Ibid.*, p. 63.

In the war of inferior against superiors Luther holds that it is not "right". As he puts it, "war and conflict with superiors cannot be right" [1].

From these passages just quoted it can be seen that Luther held really only one kind of war just, i.e., war between equals for self defense. "Self-protection is a proper cause of war and therefore all laws agree that self-defense shall go unpunished, and he who kills another in self-defense is innocent in everyone's eyes" [2]. In the matter of the war by the superior against the inferior which Luther justified, it can hardly be said that this is war in our sense of the term; it is really the exercise of police power. In these forceful words Luther sums up his position on war:

> Let this be, then, the first thing to be said on this point — War is not right, even between equal and equal, unless it is fought with such a good conscience that one can say, "My neighbor compels and forces me to fight, though I would rather avoid it". In that case, it can be called not only war, but due protection and self-defense. For a distinction must be made among wars; some are begun out of a desire and will to fight and before one is attacked, others are forced by necessity and compulsion after the attack has been made by the other party. The first kind can be called wars of desire, the second wars of necessity. The first kind are of the devil; God give him no good fortune! The second are human misfortune; God help them! [3]

Luther, of course, had little or no regard for the writings on war of the medieval churchmen and legists. His method was rather to make a loose and general statement and then to support it by a few Biblical references. His approach to the problem of the legality

---

[1] *Ibid.*, p. 56.   [2] *Ibid.*, p. 58.   [3] *Ibid.*, p. 59.

of war was religious; his speculation was the result of a rationalization of the wars of religion between the Catholic and Protestant princes.

In this period of incessant religious warfare, a very profound and light witted man — a human paradox — wrote on the social stupidity of his time. This writer was the Renaissance humanist, Desiderius Erasmus (1466–1536) [1]. Since he was concerned with most of the questions of his time, he naturally wrote on war. In his work, *The Complaint of Peace* (1521) [2], which he dedicated to Philip of Burgundy, the brother of Emperor Charles V, he discusses war in general, and makes some interesting statements on the legality of war. On the problem of the distinction between peoples with respect to war, he observes: "Nevertheless, if we must of necessity go to war, as I said before it is certainly a less evil to contend with an infidel, than christians should mutually harass and destroy their own fraternity" [3]. Erasmus wanted to preserve the peace of the European countries even at the expense of war on infidels. He did not always justify war on the infidels [4]. He was cognizant of the concept of the just war and the just cause of war, for as he writes: "Now, however, it seems to be cause enough to commence a

---

[1] Cf. Johan Huizinga, *Erasmus* (New York: C. Scribner's Sons, 1924); Lange, *op. cit.*, pp. 146–176; Preserved Smith, *Erasmus* (New York: Harper and Brothers, 1923).

[2] Erasmus, *The Complaint of Peace*, trans. by T. Paynell (Chicago: The Open Court Publishing Co., 1917).

[3] *Ibid.*, p. 56.

[4] Cf. Erasmus, *Enchiridion Militis Christiani* (Roterodamo: Lugduni Batavorum ex Officina Johannis Maire, 1504 [first pub.]).

just and necessary war, that a neighbouring land is in a more prosperous, flourishing, or free condition, than your own" [1]. Here we see Erasmus at his very best, satirizing the current notions and practices of the time on the question of the legality of war.

Another writer of the sixteenth century was Sir Thomas More (1478–1535) [2]. Although he was a contemporary of Machiavelli, Luther, and Erasmus, More was concerned with a different set of problems. Even though he was imbued with the spirit of the Renaissance, he had little sympathy for the political absolutism and materialism of his day. The social and economic evils of England More satirized cleverly in his *Utopia* (1516), a mythical land free from the ills of his own country. To some extent he was concerned with the excessive number of wars in his time and in *Utopia* he discussed what he considered the proper way of regarding war. In speaking of the Utopians, he says:

> Yet they do not rashly engage in war unless it be either to defend themselves, or their friends from any unjust aggressors, or out of good nature or in compassion assist an oppressed nation in shaking off the yoke of tyranny. They indeed help their friends not only in defensive, but also in offensive wars; but they never do that unless they had been consulted before the breach was made and being satisfied with the grounds on which they went they had

---

[1] Erasmus, *The Complaint of Peace*, p. 33.
[2] Dunning, *op. cit.*, pp. 207–209; W. E. Campbell, *More's Utopia and His Social Teaching* (London: Eyre and Spotteswoode, 1930); Engelman, *op. cit.*, pp. 136–47; Gettell, *op. cit.*, pp. 197–198; Hearnshaw, *op. cit.*, pp. 123–47; Karl Kautsky, *Thomas More and His Utopia* (London: H. & C. Black, 1927).

found that all the demands of reparation were rejected so that a war was unavoidable [1].

And More continues:

This they think to be not only just, when our neighbor makes an invasion on another, by public order, and carry away the spoils; but when the merchants of one country are oppressed in another, either under pretence of some unjust laws, or by the perverse wresting of the good ones. This they count a juster cause of war than the other, because these injuries are done under some color of laws [2].

It can be seen that More supported not only defensive war, but also in certain circumstances offensive war. He even uses the terms "defensive" and "offensive". More, however, does not justify every kind of offensive war. He holds valid only an offensive war that is waged after a consultation had been made and the demands for reparation refused. This latter qualification is very similar to the notion of Cicero [3], Dante [4], and Luther [5]. More mentions two specific just causes of war, one "when a neighbor makes an inroad on another by public order, and carry away the spoils" and the other "when the merchants of our country are oppressed in another". This latter provision which More gives as the "juster cause of war" is characteristic of his own thought and of his time. His sympathy for the merchant class is evident,

[1] More's "Utopia" in Henry Morley, *Ideal Commonwealths* (London: Colonial Press, 1901), p. 76.
[2] *Ibid.*
[3] Cf. *supra*, p. 28.
[4] Cf. *supra*, p. 40, n. 1.
[5] Cf. *supra*, p. 70.

for while he satirized English life he was politic enough to justify the current economic expansion of his country.

While More was somewhat characteristic of Tudor England, Francis Bacon (1561–1626) was a typical product of Stuart England [1]. Bacon will be discussed here instead of in the next chapter where he chronologically belongs, because of the facility of comparing him with More and Machiavelli. Bacon showed none of the liberalism that More evidenced in his works on political and social problems. On the subject of war they also differed fundamentally. While More disparaged war, Bacon favored it. Bacon writes: "No body can be healthy without exercise, neither natural body nor politic and certainly to a kingdom or estate, a just and honorable war is the true exercise, a civil war is like the heat of a fever; but a foreign war is like the heat of exercise, and serveth to keep the body in health; for in a slothful peace both courages will effeminate and manners corrupt" [2].

Bacon used the time-worn distinction between peoples with respect to war in his argument for war against the Turks. He is casuist enough to point out that it can not be based per se on the difference in religion. He writes: "Therefore in deliberations of war against the Turk, it hath been often, with equal judgment, maintained, that the Christian princes and States have always a sufficient ground of invasive war

---

[1] Gettell, *loc. cit.*

[2] Francis Bacon, *Essays*, edited by Mary A. Scott (New York: Charles Scribner's Sons, 1908), p. 143.

against the enemy; not for cause of religion; but upon a just fear; forasmuch as it is a fundamental law in the Turkish empire that they (without any other provocation) make war upon Christendom for the propagation of their law; so that there lieth upon the Christians a perpetual fear of a war (hanging over their heads) from them; and therefore they may at all times (as they think good) be upon the prevention" [1]. Bacon believed that to a certain extent a nation would always find just cause before it went to war. He interpreted just cause, however, as a rationalization necessary because of the "justice imprinted in the nature of men".

> For there is that justice imprinted in the nature of men, that they enter not upon wars (whereof so many calamities ensue) but upon some, at the least specious grounds and quarrels. The Turk hath at hand for cause of war the propagation of his law a sect, a quarrel that he may always command [2].

This passage shows us that Bacon really believed in carrying on the tradition of Machiavelli, namely, that wars are just when they exist for the reasons of state. Bacon went so far as to say that even the fear of an imminent danger was a just cause of war.

> Neither is the opinion of the schoolmen to be received, that a war cannot be made but upon a precedent injury or provocation. For there is no question but a just fear of an imminent danger though there be no blow given, is a lawful cause of war [3].

---

[1] Francis Bacon, *Works*, edited by James Spedding (London: Longman, 1874), XIV, 476.

[2] Bacon, *Essays*, p. 142.

[3] *Ibid.*, p. 86.

It is interesting to note that Bacon placed no limit upon the circumstances under which a state could make war, but this is understandable in the light of his belief in imperialism.

International Law Writers. — To the student of the history of international law, the sixteenth century is very important, as it marks the birth of modern international law. Up to this time the law of nations which had been stated by writers and publicists existed in a very inchoate and loosely defined form. There had been no professional writers on international law. In the sixteenth century the works of the international jurists appeared; the first of these were the *Relectiones* of Franciscus de Victoria (1480–1546) [1].

Paradoxical as it might seem, the age that produced Machiavelli also produced Franciscus de Victoria. The former, on the one hand, apparently had no interest in

---

[1] Gettell, *op. cit.*, p. 187; H. Hallam, *Introduction to the Literature of Europe* (New York: Harpers, 1841), I, 324–5; T. E. Holland, *Studies in International Law* (Oxford: Clarendon Press, 1898), pp. 51–2; C. Lange, *op. cit.*, pp. 269–80; E. Nys, "Introduction" in Franciscus de Victoria, *De Indis at De Jure Belli Relectiones* (Washington: Carnegie Institution, 1917); E. Nys, *Le Droit de la Guerre et les Précurseurs de Grotius* (Bruxelles et Leipzig: C. Muquardt, 1882), pp. 94–5; C. Phillipson, "Franciscus de Victoria", *Journal of Society of Comparative Legislation* (New Series; London, 1915), XV, 175; J. B. Scott, *The Spanish Origins of International Law* (Washington: Georgetown University, 1928); *The Spanish Origin of International Law; Francisco de Victoria and his Law of Nations* (Oxford: At the Clarendon Press, 1934); *The Discovery of America and Its Influences on International Law* (Washington, D. C.: Catholic University, 1929); C. Barcia Trelles, *Francisco de Victoria* (Madrid: Sección de Estudios Americanistas, 1928); Walker, *op. cit.*, pp. 214–30; H. F. Wright, *Francisci de Victoria* (Washington: H. F. Wright, 1916).

scholastic philosophy. In fact, his political theory is a practical refutation of the efficacy of scholastic philosophy. Victoria, on the other hand, continued the stream of scholastic thinking on war. Even though he was imbued with the writings of the Renaissance, he still managed to retain his Catholic viewpoint. This writer, who has been called the founder of international law by James Brown Scott, was a Spanish Dominican who occupied the chair of Sacred Theology at the University of Salamanca [1]. For some time he served as confidential adviser to King Charles V. Although Victoria was a contemporary of Machiavelli, Luther, and More, they apparently had no direct effect on his thinking. He was influenced, however, by the thought of the Renaissance; he studied under Erasmus at the University of Paris. While Machiavelli, Luther, and More paid no attention to the writings of the church-men and legists on war, Victoria kept on with the traditional approach of the schoolmen. It may be recalled that their method was to state the principle, give the arguments for and against it, using the Bible, Aristotle, and the churchmen as authorities and then to present the conclusion. With this technique Victoria attacked the political problems of his day. He was more concrete than any of the schoolmen who wrote almost exclusively on theoretical law problems. Moved by the suffering of the Indians in the New World at the hands of his fellow countrymen, Victoria became concerned with the rights and duties of the Spaniards vis à vis

---

[1] Scott, *Discovery of America and Its Influence on International Law*, p. 7.

the Indians [1]. He refreshed the scholastic thought and applied it to a new set of problems.

The writings of Victoria for which he is most renowned are *De Indis et De Jure Belli Relectiones* (*circa* 1541) [2]. The *De Indis* and the *De Juri Belli* are the two most outstanding *Relectiones* delivered by Victoria. They were lectures which he gave to his sudents at the University of Salamanca. The *De Indis* contains a discussion of, first, "what rights the Indians came under Spanish sway" and, second, "what rights the Spanish sovereigns obtained over them in temporal and civil matters", and third, "what rights their sovereign or the church obtained over them in matters spiritual and touching religion" [3]. In the *De Jure Belli* Victoria deals with four questions: first, "whether Christians make war at all"; second, "where does the authority to declare or wage war repose"; third, "what may and ought to furnish causes of just war"; and fourth, "what and how extensive measures may be taken in a just war against the enemy" [4].

As has been pointed out, the practice of this period on the distinction between peoples with respect to war was to consider the Indians of the New World as barbarians, their treatment being subject to no laws [5]. Moved by the work of Bartholomew de Las Casas who

---

[1] Cf. C. Van Vollenhoven, "Grotius and Geneve", *Bibliotheca Visseriana Dissertationum Jus-Internationale Illustrantium* (Leyden: E. J. Brill, 1926), VI, 7.

[2] Victoria, *op. cit.* (Washington: Carnegie Institution, 1917).

[3] *Ibid.*, p. 116.

[4] *Ibid.*, p. 165.

[5] Cf. *supra*, p. 62.

plead for a more humane treatment of the Indians by
the Spaniards, Victoria writes: "....if the faith be
presented to the Indians in the way named only and
they do not receive it, the Spaniards can not make this
a reason for waging war on them or for proceeding
against them under the law of war" [1]. He says further:
"This is manifest, because they are innocent in this
respect and have done no wrongs to the Spaniards" [2].
True to the traditions of scholastic philosophy Victoria
supports this statement with a quotation from St.
Augustine [3], "Accordingly, St. Augustine says (Liber
83, Questionum), 'It is involved in the definition of a
just war that some wrong is being avenged, as where a
people or state is to be punished for neglect to exact
amends from its citizens for their wrong doings or to
restore what has been wrongfully taken away'" [4]. He
also quotes St. Thomas Aquinas: "St. Thomas lays
down (Secunda Secundae, qu 40 art. 1.) 'there must be
a just cause, namely they who are attacked for some
fault must deserve the attack'" [5]. And in summary
Victoria says: "Where then, no wrong has previously
been committed by the Indians, there is no cause for a
just war" [6].

It is obvious that Victoria did not believe that the
Spaniards had a *carte blanche* to wage war against the
Indians because they were *ipso facto* infidels. He places
the Indians within the sphere of the law of war. Victoria holds, however, that if the Indians refuse to accept

---

[1] Victoria, *op. cit.*, p. 143.
[2] *Ibid.*   [3] *Ibid.*   [4] Cf. *supra*, p. 42.
[5] Victoria, *op. cit.*, p. 143.   [6] *Ibid.*

Christianity, they are guilty of "moral sin". He says, furthermore, that they are really bound to accept Christianity [1]. But he makes it clear that: "Although the Christian faith may have been announced to the Indians with adequate demonstration and they have refused to receive it, yet this is not a reason which justifies making war on them and depriving them of their property" [2]. He proves this point by citing St. Thomas Aquinas, stating that it is held by the legists, the customs of the Christian Emperors, and by saying that "war is no argument for the truth of the Christian faith" [3]. There is very little evidence in the opinion of the present writer to support Victoria in saying that the Christian Emperors by their custom did not make war on the infidels for their refusal to accept Christianity. It is worth noting that Victoria in holding that the Spaniards did not have an implicit right to wage war on the Indians probably presupposed a distinction between what was right morally and what was right legally. The Indians in refusing Christianity were wrong morally but they were not violating any principle which gave the Spaniards a cause for war.

Like Lignano, Victoria states that war is allowed not only by Natural Law but also by Divine Law [4]. Although there are in the Gospels arguments for the abstinence of Christians from war, they are to be taken as "counsel" and not as "precept" [5]. This idea is supported by the writings of the Church Fathers, the received usage of the Church, and passages in the

---

[1] *Ibid.*, p. 144. [2] *Ibid.* [3] *Ibid.*, p. 145.
[4] *Ibid.*, p. 166. [5] *Ibid.*, p. 165.

Bible [1]. Moreover since war is permitted under the Natural Law and since the Divine Law never forbids anything allowable under the Natural Law, war, most certainly, is lawful under Divine Law [2].

As to the question of the declaration of war, Victoria says, "Every state has authority to declare and to make war" [3]. He points out further that while a private person is entitled to defend what belongs to him, he cannot go out on his own to avenge a wrong done him to recover stolen property [4]. It is, however, within the rights of a state to avenge its wrongs and to recover its property [5]. He then states the proposition: "A prince has the same authority in this respect as the State has" [6].

Victoria next considers "What is a State". He answers this by saying that a state is a perfect community, one which is complete in itself and not part of another community [7]. "Such a State, then, or the prince thereof, has authority to declare war, and no one else" [8]. Although anyone can wage defensive war, only states or princes can wage offensive war [9]. Defensive war is more inclusive because, since force is naturally repelled by force, anyone has the right of self-defense without any authority [10]. The waging of offensive war is reserved exclusively for states or princes because states have moral obligations to perform in the society of states, while persons are not

---

[1] *Ibid.*   [2] *Ibid.*, p. 166.   [3] *Ibid.*, p. 168.
[4] *Ibid.*   [5] *Ibid.*   [6] *Ibid.*
[7] *Ibid.*, p. 169.   [8] *Ibid.*   [9] *Ibid.*, pp. 168–9.
[10] *Ibid.*, p. 167.

supposed to invoke the Divine Law and the Natural Law to mete out punishment [1]. This concept of the interdependence of states with reciprocal rights and duties seems to be an original one, and in this light, some scholars give Victoria credit for the invention of the concept of "jus inter gentes" [2].

As to a classification of wars into offensive and defensive, Victoria, it seems, carries on the doctrine of Lignano, namely, that anyone has the right of waging defensive war, but only the state or the prince has the right of waging offensive war. In the composition of the latter category, Victoria brings into use the concept of the multiplicity of states. Lignano, may it be repeated, held that there was really only one state, which was the Empire with the overlordship of the papacy, but Victoria holds that there are many states which are headed by many different princes who are supreme in their own political powers [3]. The former maintained that only the papacy in the last analysis has the power to declare war; while the latter writer holds that each of these princes has the power to declare war, since they are the legal agents of the states [4].

It is seen then that one of the requisites for a just war, if it is an offensive war, is that it must be declared by a prince. It must also have a just cause. As Victoria writes: "There is a single and only just cause for com-

---

[1] *Ibid.*, pp. 168–9.
[2] Cf. Introduction by E. Nys, *op. cit.*, p. 11.
[3] *De Indis et De Jure Belli Relectiones*, p. 168.
[4] *Ibid.*, p. 167.

mencing a war, namely, a wrong received" [1]. This means that in order to have a just cause of war, the state which is doing the attacking must have received some injury from the state which is being attacked. This is precisely the same doctrine which was expressed by Saint Augustine over one thousand years previous to its restatement by Victoria. And as such it is acknowledged by Victoria [2]. It means that if no wrong has been received by a state, there is no need of vengeance, and hence no war [3]. He attempts to prove this by the following syllogism: since a prince has no greater authority over foreigners than over his own subjects, and since he cannot "draw his sword" against his own subjects unless they have done some wrong, he cannot wage war against other princes' subjects unless they have done him some wrong [4].

Victoria does not directly refer to unjust causes of war, but he does so indirectly by stating that there are some things which are not just causes of war. These are (1) differences in religion, (2) extensions of empires, and (3) personal ambitions of princes [5]. In the first category he compromises the doctrine held in his time that Christians have a natural right to wage war on infidels, particularly the Indians in the New World by saying that when the infidels refuse to give a hearing to Christians, they do them no injury provoking war, but are guilty of "mortal sin" [6]. In the second category he states that the principle is too well

---

[1] *Ibid.*, p. 170.
[2] *Ibid.*, and cf. *supra*, p. 80.
[3] *Ibid.*   [4] *Ibid.*, p. 171.   [5] *Ibid.*, p. 170.
[6] *Ibid.*, p. 144.

known to need further proof [1]. And in the third category he argues by another syllogism. A prince derives his authority from the state which wants him to increase the common good to its fullest extent, and all decisions must be advantageous to the common good; therefore, a decision to wage war must be made for the common good and not for the personal advantage of the prince [2].

Since the prince has the sole power of declaring war, he has an enormous control over the destiny of his state. This is partially limited by the rule laid down by Victoria that, although the prince has the sole power of declaring war, he has not the exclusive control over the determination of a just cause which is necessary for a lawful or just war. In order to ascertain the justness of a particular cause of war, the prince must consult "God and the Wise" [3]. And when an opinion is reached as to whether or not the particular cause is a just one, it must come up to "the standard of the wise man's judgment, as appears from Ethics, [Aristotle] bk. 2" [4].

When the justness of a particular war is doubtful, as evidenced by each side claiming that it has a just cause, resort should be made, according to Victoria, to a compromise and not to war [5]. A war, however, cannot be just on both sides [6]. But because of "invincible ignorance", ignorance of law or fact, one side might think it to be just [7]. He says: "There is no inconsist-

---

[1] *Ibid*., p. 170.   [2] *Ibid*.
[3] *Ibid*., p. 173.   [4] *Ibid*.
[5] *Ibid*., p. 175.   [6] *Ibid*., p. 177.   [7] *Ibid*.

ency, indeed, in holding the war to be a just war on both sides, seeing that on one side there is right and on the other side there is invincible ignorance" [1]. This is illustrated by the case of the French holding the province of Burgundy with "demonstrable ignorance" in the belief that it belongs to them, while the right of Charles V to it is certain. He may make a just war to regain it, while the French may justly defend it [2]. As two students of the subject have put it: ".... by a rapid transition Victoria widened the whole basis of discussion by expanding the canonical 'invincible ignorance' into a novel 'excusable [demonstrable, Latin, *probabile*] ignorance', a step which widened out of all knowledge the number of wars which could be regarded as just on both sides" [3].

This is the essence of Victoria's doctrines on the just cause of war. His major assumption is that there are fundamental rights and wrongs which emanate from the Divine Law and the Natural Law. By the application of a cause of war to this system of rights and

[1] *Ibid.*, p. 155.

[2] *Ibid.*

[3] Butler and Maccoby, *op. cit.*, p. 114: "Molina (1535–1600) pushed to their logical conclusion the consequences of Victoria's admission. 'If two parties are of different opinions and each one believes without doubt that the object of the strife belongs to him obviously one of the two parties is deceived, but if his error be invincible in that he has applied the proper diligence and has followed the advice of experienced men, the war will be just on both sides'". Regout, *op. cit.*, p. 261, refutes the position that some modern scholars take on showing that Molina believed that a war can be just on both sides. The present writer finds himself on this question to be in agreement with Butler and Maccoby, *op. cit.*, p. 114, and with Vanderpol, *op. cit.*, p. 253 with whom Regout disagrees.

wrongs wars would be decreased because states cannot act contrary to the Divine Law and the Natural Law and survive. Such are his postulates.

The significance of Victoria on the problem of the legality of war lies in his application of the long used scholastic method to the society of states which comprised Europe in the sixteenth century. He saw a system of rights and duties emanating from a crudely constructed Divine Law and Natural Law which was beginning to put some order into a chaos that reigned in Europe. Although he did not work out any notions of neutrality and the duty of third states to go to war or distinguish any limitations on war with respect to time and place, he has given us some of the earliest cryptic ideas on the declaration of war by the sovereign and an almost faultless analysis of just causes of war.

A compilation of the ideas and concepts of preceeding writers coupled with a collection of customs and practices of states was the famous treatise, *De Jure et Officilis Bellicis et Disciplina Militari Libri III*, 1582. This was the work of Balthazar Ayala (1548–84) [1], another of the early writers on international law. Although it is not outstanding for its originality, the work is an interesting example of the importance of certain doctrines held during the latter part of the sixteenth century.

---

[1] He was military auditor (Judge Advocate) for the Spanish armies in the Netherlands. For biographical sketch see "Introduction" by John Westlake in Ayala, *De Jure et Officilis Bellicis et Disciplina Militari Libri III* (Washington, D. C.: Carnegie Institution, 1912), Vol. I.

On the question of the distinction between peoples with respect to war Ayala reaches the same conclusion that Victoria did. He says: "War may not be declared against infidels merely because they are infidels, not even on the authority of the Emperor or Pope, for their infidel character does not divest them of those rights of ownership which they have under the law universal jus gentium" [1]. It is obvious from the passage quoted above that Ayala did not believe that the *jus gentium* applied only to the Christians and that therefore the Spaniards could make war on the infidels.

On the procedure for declaring war Ayala reviews only the Roman practice of the fetial college. He does not state clearly that the sovereign prince has the right to declare war. In fact, if a war is to be just, it must be declared by the authority of the prince [2]. This implies that private warfare is prohibited because no person except the sovereign can undertake war as a means of settling disputes. By the *Lex Regia* the people have conferred solely on the prince the right to declare war [3]. However the prince's exclusive authority to declare war does not extend to defensive war, which the Law of Nature permits anyone to wage [4]. In emergency situations necessitating immediate action, war may be commenced without the authority of the prince [5]. It seems that this principle not only includes the right of a state to ward off an attack by another

---

[1] *Ibid.*, English translation by John Pawley Bate (Washington, D. C.: Carnegie Institution, 1912), II, 21.

[2] *Ibid.*, p. 9.   [3] *Ibid.*

[4] *Ibid.*, p. 10.   [5] *Ibid.*, p. 9.

state, but also encompasses the right of a state in anticipating an attack to take the initial military action. This would be an offensive war which would be for defensive purposes. The doctrine of justice seems to be subservient to the doctrine of expediency.

In most offensive wars notwithstanding the unusual exception noted above, it is necessary that they be declared by the authority of the prince, if they are to be just wars. Besides this requisite, they must possess just causes [1]. The basis of a just cause of war is a wrong which a state receives; this wrong may be manifested by thefts from a state, or insults to it [2]. Ayala does not directly refer to unjust causes of war, but since he positively refers to just causes, he negatively acquiesces in that there are also unjust causes.

In summary, it may be said that a just war, according to Ayala, is one which is declared by the authority of the prince, and must possess a just cause. He points out that if only the legality of a declaration of war were the sole criterion of the justness of war, a war would be "just" on both sides, provided that it were properly declared [3]. But since the justness of the cause of an offensive war is another essential criterion of its justness, an offensive war can never be "just" on both sides because only one side can possess the just cause or causes [4]. This principle goes back to the absolutistic doctrines of rights and wrongs which were stated by Victoria.

On the question of the attitude of third states with

---

[1] *Ibid.*, p. 10.   [2] *Ibid.*, p. 11.
[3] *Ibid.*, pp. 22–23.   [4] *Ibid.*

respect to a war, Ayala leans toward the position that third states should not remain neutral, but should join the state with the just cause of war [1].

In general, Ayala is very similar to Victoria in his doctrines of just war and unjust causes of war. Both of them were Spaniards, both lived in the sixteenth century, and both of them believed in a philosophy of natural law and absolutistic rights. Though the former was a Judge Advocate, and the latter, a professor of sacred theology, the difference in their conclusions is scarcely noticeable. Since Victoria preceded Ayala by one generation, Ayala probably drew very heavily upon Victoria for his doctrines of just war and just causes of war.

The last of the Spanish school of writers on international law to be presented is Franciscus Suarez (1548–1617) [2]. He has been styled "the last of the Schoolmen" [3]. Like Victoria he was a theologian who wrote on law [4]. While Victoria was a member of the Dominican order, Suarez was a Jesuit. His most

---

[2] *Ibid.*, p. 20.

[1] Cf. Dunning, *Luther to Montesquieu*, pp. 132–52; Hallam, *op. cit.*, p. 141; P. V. Masterson *et al.*, *Francisco Suarez, Addresses in Commemoration of His Contribution to International Law and Politics* (Washington: H. F. Wright, 1933); H. Rommen, *Die Staatslehre des Franz Suarez*, S. J. (M. Gladbach, 1926); J. B. Scott, *Spanish Origin of International Law*; F. W. Sherwood, "Francisco Suarez", *Transactions of the Grotius Society* (London: Sweet and Maxwell, 1927), XII, 19–31; C. B. Trelles, "Francisco Suarez", *Hague. Academie de Droit International. Recueil des Cours* (Paris: Librairie du Recueil Sirey, 1933), XLIII (1932), 43, 389–549; A. Vanderpol, *op. cit.*, pp. 360–361; E. Plappart, *Franz Suarez als Völkerrechtler* (Darmstadt: Edward Roether, 1914).

[3] T. A. Walker, *op. cit.*, 155–156.

[4] He was a professor in the University of Coimbra, Portugal.

famous work is the *Tractatus de Legibus ac Deo Legislatore* (1612). The work of Victoria was a statement of the law which the Spaniards should use in dealing with the Indians in the New World; the writings of Ayala were concerned with the laws of war applicable to the revolt in the Low Countries. But this work of Suarez is the apotheosis of the Spanish school without any specific political application [1].

In the last of the works of Suarez, *Opus de triplici virtute theologica* (1621), there is a disputation on war [2]. Like Victoria and Ayala, Suarez believed that no nation had a right to go to war against infidels because of the fact that they were infidels [3]. In other words he made no crude distinction between peoples with respect to war. The declaration of war could be made only by the legitimate authority. It is the sovereign prince who has this legitimate authority [4]. "The power of declaring war is a kind of jurisdictional power, and the *acts included within it* belong to punitive justice, which is especially necessary in a State for purpose of constraining wrongdoers" [5]. His notion of the sovereign is interesting.

> It may be replied, first, that all kings in the respect are sovereign.... Many dukes also claim this sovereign power. Hence some of the canonists are mistaken in saying that only the Empire is sovereign in this fashion. [6]

---

[1] Scott, *op. cit.*, p. 74.

[2] Vanderpol has translated into French the disputation on war. It is found in Vanderpol, *op. cit.*, pp. 362–412.

[3] *Ibid.*, p. 233.

[4] *Ibid.*, p. 368.

[5] Quoted in Scott, *op. cit.*, p. 78.

[6] *Ibid.*, p. 79.

It is worth mentioning at this point that Suarez went much further than Victoria by pointing out specifically that the Empire was not the only sovereign power. At the time of Victoria the Emperor and the King of Spain were the same person, Charles V.

By virtue of his right to declare war, the prince has to act as an accuser and as a judge. He has to proffer charges against a wrongdoing state after he has judged the merits of the own case. A war cannot be just unless it has a just cause and is necessary [1]. A just cause of war is an injury received. This is the typical scholastic definition. The injury may be of three different kinds, (1) the foreign prince refusing to restore something that is not his, (2) the foreign prince refusing communal things, according to the *jus gentium*, as passage through public highways, reciprocal commerce, etc., (3) the foreign prince committing an offense against his esteem or honour [2].

Suarez treats the question of the justice of war on both sides. He opines that it is impossible for a war to be just on both sides except in the case of ignorance [3]. This is very much the same idea as that held by Victoria. It throws the question open further: how can the ignorance be measured? This brings us to the Probabilist Theory associated with the name of Molina. If, after a complete examination of his cause of war, the sovereign decided that right was more probable on his side, he could then declare war. But if he decided that the right was more probable on the side of his

---

[1] Vanderpol, *op. cit.*, p. 378.
[2] *Ibid.*, p. 379.   [3] *Ibid.*, p. 390.

adversary, he could not declare war [1]. It might be mentioned in passing that in cases of doubt the prince should consult the grandees of the State; but upon the question of whether or not he should take their advice, he was the sole judge [2].

Since most of the wars of his day were fought over the title to property, Suarez said that in a case where neither of the disputants occupied the territory and both were claiming it, resort could be made to arbitration by arbiters selected by the two sovereigns [3]. This, however, he said was but rarely done.

Victoria, Ayala, and Saurez all considered the legal position of war by the use of the technique of scholastic philosophy. In their attempt to control war, these writers relied to a considerable extent upon the works of the Church Fathers. The break away from the scholastic approach to this problem was yet to be accomplished. This was done by an Italian who had been sometime a professor of law at Oxford University. Alberico Gentili (1552–1608) [4] profoundly changed the course of writing on international law. One of his staunch admirers, Professor T. E. Holland, has summed up very well the achievement of Gentili:

---

[1] *Ibid.*, pp. 389–90. [2] *Ibid.*, p. 392.
[3] *Ibid.*, pp. 391–392.
[4] An Italian Protestant exile who was Regius Professor of Civil Law at Oxford. Cf. F. F. Abbott, "Alberico Gentili and His Advocatio Hispanica", *AJIL*, X (1916), 737–48; Holland, *Studies in International Law* (Oxford: Clarendon Press, 1898), pp. 1–23; C. Phillipson, "Introduction" in Gentili. *De Jure Belli Libri Tres* (Oxford: Clarendon Press, 1933), II, 9a–51a; Walker, *op. cit.*, pp. 249–276.

His achievement was threefold. He got rid of questions
of tactics and of the discipline of armies; he reduced to
reasonable dimensions the topic of private warfare; and
he placed the subject on a non-theological basis [1].

His best known work is *De Jure Belli* which appeared
in 1589. The method which he employed was more
realistic than any of the other acknowledged writers
on international law, for, although he used as authorities the Bible, classical writers, and even natural law,
he resorted to contemporary practice as a source of
law. What he did was to examine the concrete facts
and from them deduce a general rule which could be
applied, modified, or even canceled in accordance with
new conditions. He has been called by some the real
father of international law.

Gentili defines war as follows: "War is a just and
public contest of arms" [2]. The fact that it is a "public
contest" implies that it is waged by sovereigns who
are equals [3]. "A state of war does not exist with pirates
and robbers" [4]. He says also that "With pirates and
brigands, who violate all laws no laws remain in
force" [5]. It is worth nothing here that Gentili pointed
out that the law of nations did not apply to those who
revolted [6]. On the question of whether or not a difference in religion gave a sovereign the right to make war,
Gentili's answer is in the negative [7]. He believes that
the widely practiced distinction between peoples with

---

[1] Holland, *op. cit.*, p. 58.
[2] *De Jure Belli Libri Tres* (Oxford: Clarendon Press, 1933), II,
12.
[3] *Ibid.*   [4] *Ibid.*, p. 22.   [5] *Ibid.*, p. 24.
[6] Cf. *Ibid.*, pp. 24–25.   [7] Cf. *Ibid.*, pp. 43–45.

respect to war is not founded on anything natural. The unity of all men in one class makes this notion false [1].

The problem of the declaration concerned Gentili. He wrote: "And this justice of which we speak seems in the first place to consist in this: that we should inform of our deliberations the one against whom we have decided to make war" [2]. A war must have a formal declaration [3]. For this proposition Gentili quotes Cicero. He does admit that under certain circumstances war need not be formally declared. One of these is in the case where war is undertaken for "necessary defense" [4]. Another is in the case of "expedient defense" [5]. When a state receives an injury which is of a "warlike kind", war does not have to be declared [6]. He also says: ".... war will not be declared upon those who are already regarded as enemies" [7]. "Moreover, war is waged without being declared, if the acts of injustice are continued or are still going on" [8]. War does not have to be declared in a situation where "a chief makes war on a beneficiary or feudal subject" [9]. This is also the same in dealing with rebels — no declaration is required [10]. "But if war is not declared then war is said to be carried on treacherously and such a war is unjust, detestable, and savage" [11].

As has been pointed out Gentili defined war as a "just and public contest of arms" [12]. This definition has three elements: the first is that it is a public contest

---

[1] *Ibid.*, p. 69.   [2] *Ibid.*, p. 131.   [3] *Ibid.*
[4] *Ibid.*, p. 136.   [5] *Ibid.*   [6] *Ibid.*, pp. 136–7.
[7] *Ibid.*, p. 137.   [8] *Ibid.*   [9] *Ibid.*, p. 138.
[10] *Ibid.*, p. 139.   [11] *Ibid.*, p. 140.   [12] Cf. *supra*, p. 94.

between sovereigns. By this he means that since sovereigns have no earthly judge, it is inevitable that sovereigns use war as the means of making a decision [1]. As he writes: "Furthermore, private individuals, subject peoples and petty sovereigns are never confronted with the necessity of resorting to the arbitrament of Mars, since they can obtain their legal rights before their superiors tribunal" [2]. The second element in his definition is that war exists by the force of arms. And the third element is that war must be just, that is, commenced and conducted in a just fashion according to the laws of nations. The justification of war is based on necessity. He says: "Therefore, I conclude that unless it is necessary, war cannot be just since a just war is said to be declared as a result of necessity" [3].

There are three kinds of just causes of war: those that are of divine, natural, or human origin [4]. Under the first category, he places the express commands of God, as in the case of the orders to the Jews. Natural causes of war have been held as in the case of the Greeks against the barbarians, of the Christians against the infidels, and of the Spaniards against the Indians. Gentili believed that all this was on a false basis, for he regarded mankind as a natural unity [5]. Under natural causes justifying war Gentili says: "Now although I maintain that no natural cause of war exists, yet there are reasons because of which we undertake wars under Nature's guidance" [6].

He proceeds to discuss wars undertaken by necessary

---

[1] *De Jure Belli*, p. 15.   [2] *Ibid.*, p. 20.   [3] *Ibid.*
[4] *Ibid.*, p. 35.   [5] *Ibid.*, p. 54.   [6] *Ibid.*, p. 58.

defense or immediate defense [1]. There is also expedient defense when war is precipitated by the fear of attack [2]. As he writes: "A defense is just which anticipates dangers that are already meditated and prepared, and also those which are not meditated, but are probable and possible" [3]. Here is an interesting illustration of the application of the doctrine of the "balance of power" idea. There remains among the kinds of defense which Gentili justifies, defense for the sake of honour. Since the whole world is one body, and all men are members of that body, states are obligated to help the injured state [4].

After having listed the various forms of just causes for defensive war, Gentili proceeds to inquire into those for offensive war. These are, necessity, expediency, and honor — the same as the defensive causes. Necessity is understood in the sense that a state cannot maintain its existance without it [5]. An example of this is the interference with the excess population of a state occupying vacant territory. "An expedient cause for making war will be the right of taking vengeance for a wrong which one has suffered" [6]. Examples of this are avenging justice received, in order to make the commission of others impossible, and vindicating the

---

[1] *Ibid.*   [2] *Ibid.*, p. 61.   [3] *Ibid.*, p. 66.

[4] *Ibid.*, p. 69: "And since we are one body, just as the other members would aid the one that was injured, if one member should desire to harm another, since it is for the interest of the whole body, even of the offending member, that each of the members be preserved: exactly so men will aid one another, since security cannot be maintained except by the love and protection of those who compose it".

[5] *Ibid.*, p. 79.   [6] *Ibid.*, p. 83.

refusal of certain rights as harbouring, trading, and the right of passage. The last form of a just cause for an offensive war is honour. This is existent in a condition where certain practices are against common decency and honor; i.e., people indulging in bestial vice [1].

The last category of the reasons for making war is that of wars justified by the human reason. We have so far discussed those emanating from divine and natural reason. Gentili used the expression "human reason" to include the case "when war is resorted to because of the violation of some man-made law" [2]. In other words, there must be an offense committed against some positive rights [3]. It must be not a trivial violation, but a very important one.

Gentili, like Victoria and Suarez, was concerned with the question of whether or not war can be just on both sides. He believed that it could be, provided that there was "reasonable doubt as to the justice of the cause" [4]. As he states it: "It is the nature of wars for both sides to maintain that they are supporting a just cause. In general, it may be true that in nearly every kind of dispute that neither of the two disputants is unjust" [5]. And later on he says: "But it is doubtful on which side justice is, and if each side aims at justice, neither can be called unjust" [6]. On the question of one side having a more just cause than the other, Gentili says that the greater justice of the cause of the opponent does not detract from the justice of the cause of the sovereign [7].

---

[1] *Ibid.*, p. 122.   [2] *Ibid.*, p. 93.   [3] *Ibid.*
[4] *Ibid.*, p. 31.   [5] *Ibid.*   [6] *Ibid.*, p. 32.
[7] *Ibid.*, p. 33.

It is evident that Gentili had a clear comprehension of the notion of territorial sovereignty [1]. This is implied in his treatise, *Hispanicae advocationis libri duo* (1605) [2]. His conception of neutrality was quite modern. In this treatise he displayed a knowledge of neutral rights and duties emanating from the principle of territorial sovereignty. On the problem of the duty of third states with respect to war, Gentili makes some interesting comments. As has already been pointed out by the present writer [3], he listed under the heading of the just cause for defensive war, honor. By this Gentili meant the right of a third state to go to war against a state which was an unjust aggressor against still another state. It must be noted, however, that third states held this only as a right; they were not bound to do so. In a case where two allies of a state are at war with each other, Gentili holds that the third state should refuse to give aid to the state which does not have the just cause [4].

The present writer has failed to find any limitations on war with respect to place. There is, however, a time limitation on war which Gentili distinguishes. It is the old Roman practice of a thirty-three day period elapsing between the declaration of war and the beginning of hostilities [5].

Summary. — The practice and theory of the

---

[1] Walker, *op. cit.*, p. 274.

[2] Gentili, *Hispanices advocationis libri duo* (1605) (New York: Oxford Press, 1921).

[3] Cf. *supra*, p. 97.

[4] *De Jure Belli*, II, 391.

[5] *Ibid.*, p. 135.

position of war in international law had an interesting development during the fifteenth and sixteenth centuries. With the decay of the feudal system and the decline of the power of the Emperor and the Pope, there came into being an international anarchy out of which grew the system of balance of power. During this period struggles took place between the European nations and the Turks and between Spain and the Indians. This gave rise to a more clear statement that in theory there was no distinction between peoples with respect to war, even through the practice was otherwise. In theory Victoria, the Spanish Dominican, worked it out most completely, while Suarez, the Spanish Jesuit, Ayala, the Spanish judge and advocate, and Gentili, the Oxford professor, restated the distinction, but added nothing further.

In an age of absolute monarchy one would naturally expect the writers of the day to hold that only the sovereign was qualified to declare war. All of them believed this to be the legal procedure. Aside from the question of who can declare war, the writers, with the exception of Ayala, were not concerned with a discussion of the actual means of declaring war. In the fifteenth and sixteenth centuries there were still instances of declaring war by means of a herald.

The practice of the time had an effect upon the direction of the thinking concerning the just and unjust causes of war. Since it was the sovereign's right to declare war, it was also his duty to decide whether or not a war was just. Machiavelli made it a simple task for the sovereign, for the latter had merely to decide whether or not the war was necessary for the reason of state. If a war was necessary, it was just. The position of Luther on the question of just war was that only sovereigns could make war, and that the only war which was just was a war of necessity. Luther's conception of necessity was much different from that of Machiavelli. He held that a war was necessary when a neighbor makes an attack. In other words, it had to be for self-defense. Machiavelli's notion of necessity was that a war is necessary when it is for the utility of the state. More, however, justified not only defensive war but also offensive war. He defines a defensive war as one originating out of an invasion or some unjust aggression. The only valid kind of offensive war is one made after consultation and after the demands for reparation have been refused. This was also enunciated by Luther. It is interesting to note that it bears some resemblance to a definition of war by Professor Shotwell [1]. Erasmus satirized the frequency of wars of his day and even the concept of the just war. The ideas of Bacon on just war and the just causes of war were virtually the same as those of Machiavelli. Wars are just when they exist for reasons of state.

The Spanish writers, Victoria, Ayala, and Suarez all stated that a war is just if it is declared by the sovereign and has a just cause. A just cause, they said, is a wrong received. This is the old Ciceronian concept. Gentili's notion of the just cause of war was quite

---

[1] Cf. J. T. Shotwell, *War as an Instrument of National Policy* (New York: Harcourt Brace & Co., 1929).

different from that of his predecessors. He believed that wars can be just whether they are defensive or offensive, each one having a set of just causes.

It should be pointed out here that all of these representative writers on war in the fifteenth and sixteenth centuries were rationalizing the politics of the time. The period was one of dynastic expansion. A frequent cause of war was the desire to acquire territory. While the churchmen and legists of the Middle Ages sought the *bonum commune*, the writers of the fifteenth and sixteenth centuries sought the interests of their Sovereign. In mediaeval times the determination of the just cause of war was dependent upon the power of the Emperor and the Pope, as well as upon the moral influence of the Church. With the passing of feudalism the theory of the just cause of war continued but its determination was no longer dependent upon the Pope and Emperor. It was entrusted to the Sovereign. As has been mentioned, it was the Sovereign who decided what were the just causes of war. The mediaeval theory rested upon the assumption that the just cause of war was easily ascertained; a sharply contrasted justice and injustice existed in the normal case. In other words, there could be only one just cause in a dispute. Victoria, Suarez, Ayala, and Gentili were somewhat favorably disposed to the idea that a war could be just on both sides, since, through "invincible ignorance", it might be impossible to find the really just cause. The notion of the mediaeval schoolmen on a just war — guilt on one side and righteousness on the other —

practically vanished. There came in its place the idea
that the Sovereign was to make war as an accuser and
as a judge. The possibility that a war may be just on
both sides was discussed by these writers. While they
stated that a war could not be just on both sides, they
widened by casuistry the chances for making virtually
any kind of war just. They were imbued with the idea
of the "Reason of State".

With the system of the balance of power the notion
of neutrality became a more essential part of European
diplomacy. The treaties, particularly those made by
the Italian city-states, afforded a crude beginning of a
kind of multi-lateral treaty which obligated the
signatories to keep peace among themselves, and if
one of them broke the peace with any other, to allow
the remaining states to go to war against the recalcitrant state. Through the practice of neutralizing
certain areas there was a limitation on the place of
making war. In a sense the whole system of the balance
of power was a means of limiting the time of waging
war, because it created a series of treaties which were
designated for a certain period of years within which
there was to be peace between the signatories.

The writers were beginning to regard international
law as a cohesive force in joining together more
amicably the states of the world. Particular mention
should be made of the broadening of the definitions of
the *jus gentium*. Along with this went the idea that
there was an international society which required of a
state certain duties. This is most specific in the writings
of Gentili who held that the world is one body, that

states are all members of that body, and hence that they are obligated to help an injured state. In concluding it must be pointed out that this was, nevertheless, an age of absolutism in which each state was struggling for power and prestige. The writers on international law were natural products of this period; they reflected the spirit of the time in their writings and they easily justified the practice of their states in precise legalistic theory.

CHAPTER IV

THE SEVENTEENTH CENTURY

Practice. — The transition from the sixteenth to the seventeenth century was marked by the existence of another paradox. While professional international law writers were laying down rules limiting the international conduct of states, political theorists like Bodin (1530–1596) had begun to formulate the principles of unlimited nationalism. This phenomenon paved the way for power politics on the international level.

The modern European state system was fully established by the Peace of Westphalia [1] which marked the end of the Thirty Years' War. This was a continuation of the wars of religion which plagued the preceding century. It was a European struggle distinguished by much bitterness, by long duration, but at least by the fulfillment of peace. As has been pointed out in the preceding chapter, the system of the balance of power grew out of the break-down of feudalism. It was not fully matured until the seventeenth century. The European state system was to endure a long time, as there was nothing to disturb it. Its existence was threatened, however, by Louis XIV. The *Grand Monarque* attempted to extend the boundaries of France

---

[1] R. B. Mowat, *European States System* (London: Oxford University Press, 1923).

but was foiled in his efforts by the consolidated opposition of certain other states.

In the seventeenth century the problem of distinguishing peoples with respect to war did not seem very important. The problem of declaring war was ever present. With the use of printed papers came the practice of sending a printed declaration of war. This was done in 1671 by the English King in his war against the Dutch [1]. As soon as there were permanent embassies, the practice of a printed declaration of war became decadent. In the seventeenth century there were few instances of wars opening without a declaration, as in the case of the invasion of Germany in 1630 by Gustavus Adolphus [2]. It can be pointed out here that the practice of a sovereign declaring a war continued. Absolute monarchs still ruled. The only exception to this was in England after the Revolution of 1688 but it did not alter the British procedure of declaring war. By the seventeenth century there is evidence to show that sovereigns were inquiring into the causes of their wars, in order to determine whether they were just or unjust. "In the seventeenth century it gradually became clear that, if war was raging between any two states, those states which took no part in the war had peculiar rights against, and owed peculiar duties to, the states at war with one another" [3]. Due to the fact that during the sixteenth and early part of the seventeenth centuries Europe was torn by

---

[1] Holland, *Lectures*, p. 252.
[2] *Ibid.*, p. 253.
[3] Holdsworth, *op. cit.*, V, 43.

religious wars, national interest did not exclusively dominate the foreign policy of states. It was not until after the Peace of Westphalia that particular political interests took precedence over religious issues in the relations between the states. Only when the religious wars were concluded could neutrality be practiced. It was the question of neutral rights as to shipping which made the British declare war on the French and Dutch in the latter part of the seventeenth century [1]. There was then the practice of neutrality, but no well defined duty of third states to go to war. It is difficult to find any limitations on war with respect to time and place. On the whole what the seventeenth century contributed toward the practice of international law was not the addition of anything new to the problem of the legality of war, but rather the development of new sets of minor problems which gave rise to new practices between states. These became traditionalized into what is known as the international law of peace. War was, nevertheless, a subject which was very much on the minds of the thinkers of the day.

International Law Writers. — The foremost writer on the subject of war during the seventeenth century was Hugo Grotius (1583–1645) [2], who has been called

[1] G. N. Clark, *The Seventeenth Century* (Oxford: Clarendon Press, 1929), p. 131.
[2] Elemér Balough, "The Traditional Element in Grotius' Conception of International Law", *New York University Law Quarterly Review*, Vol. VII (1930), No. 2, p. 277; G. N. Clark, *op. cit.*, pp. 125–27; Dunning, *op. cit.*, pp. 153–91; Gettell, *op. cit.*, pp. 189–92; Pieter Geyl, "Grotius", *Transactions of the Grotius Society* (London: Sweet and Maxwell, 1927), XII, 81–97; Hallam, *op. cit.*, II, 141–62; Rudolf Helm, *Hugo Grotius* (Rostock: H. Warkenstiens, 1920);

108 THE SEVENTEENTH CENTURY

the father of international law. Although the paternity
of international law belongs as much to Victoria and
Gentili, yet Grotius is still considered the most
significant writer on international law. Born in Holland, exiled to France, and employed for some time
by Sweden, he was truly an international person. At
the age of twenty-one he wrote his *De Jure Praedae*.
This work prepared for the Dutch East Indies Company was a refutation of the Portuguese claim to the
East Indies. The Dutch East Indies Company was
carrying on war against the Portuguese. Grotius
justified this in his *De Jure Praedae*. At an early age
one of the chapters of this work was published — the

Holdsworth, *op. cit.*, V, 25–60; W. S. M. Knight, "Hugo Grotius",
Transactions of the Grotius Society (London: Sweet and Maxwell,
1920), VI, 1–24; Knight, *Life and Works of Hugo Grotius* (London:
Sweet and Maxwell, 1925); Lange, *op. cit.*, pp. 306–325; C. E. Mer-
riam, *History of the Theory of Sovereignty since Rousseau* (New York:
Columbia University, 1900), pp. 21–24; Jacob Ter Meulen, *Bei-
trag zur Geschichte der Internationalen Organisation 1300–1700*
(Haag: Martinus Nijhoff, 1916), pp. 107–13; E. Nys, *Les Origines*;
Roscoe Pound, "Grotius in the Science of Law", *AJIL*, XIX (1925),
685–8; James Brown Scott, "Grotius' De Jure Belli ac Pacis: The
Work of a Lawyer, Statesman, and Theologian", *AJIL*, XIX
(1925), 461–8; Scott, "Introduction" in *De Jure Belli ac Pacis*,
Translated by Francis W. Kelsey (Oxford: Clarendon Press, 1925),
II, ix-xlii; C. Van Vollenhoven, "Grotius and Geneva", *Bibliotheca
Visseriana* Leyden: E. J. Brill, 1926), VI, 544; Van Vollenhoven,
"Grotius and the Study of Law", *AJIL*, XIX (1925), 1–11; Van
Vollenhoven, *On the Genesis of the De Jure Belli et Pacis* (Grotius,
1625) (Amsterdam: Koninklijke Akademie, 1924); Van Vollenho-
ven, *The Three States in the Evolution of the Law of Nations* (The
Hague: Martinus Nijhoff, 1919); H. Vreeland, *Hugo Grotius* (New
York: Oxford Univ. Press, 1917); Walker, *op. cit.*, pp. 278–337;
John Westlake, *Collected Papers*, Edited by L. Oppenheim (Cam-
bridge: University Press, 1914), pp. 36–51; A. D. White, *Seven
Great Statesmen* (New York: Century, 1910), pp. 53–110.

Mare Liberum (1609). Not only was this work a challenge to the Portuguese but also to the English who were contending for a *mare clausum*. The dispute between Holland and Great Britain over the fishing rights, particularly in Greenland, was another case where the Dutch drew heavily upon the skill of Grotius. His most famous work is the *De Jure Belli ac Pacis* (1625). After having been involved in religious controversy in his native country, Grotius fled to France where he wrote this celebrated treatise. The fact that he assembled it in the midst of the Thirty Years' War is of no little importance. It is obvious that he wrote this work to check the ever increasing desire of princes and people to wage arbitrary and incessant wars.

The international anarchy which began in the fifteenth century continued through the seventeenth century. It was in the seventeenth century that people realized that the international lawlessness prevailed everywhere. Unlike Victoria, Ayala, Suarez, and Gentili, Grotius wrote a complete statement of what he thought the existing law was. The greatness of his *De Jure Belli ac Pacis* does not lie in its originality but in its thorough compilation of what had already been written on the subject of international law. He also drew heavily upon his *De Jure Praedae* which he had prepared many years before.

Before proceeding with the ideas of Grotius on the legality of war, it is necessary to establich in our minds the Grotian system of international law. Writers like Victoria and Suarez held that natural law was some-

thing different from the *jus gentium*. The latter was
conventional and traditional. War according to
Suarez was a historical fact, while to Grotius it was a
legal right. The author of *De Jure Belli ac Pacis* arrived
at this idea by fusing natural law with the *jus gentium*.
He made the latter a direct consequence of the former.
Natural law is the basis of his system. He defines
natural law as follows: "The law of nature is a dictate
of right reason, which points out that an act, according as it is or is not in conformity with rational nature,
has in it a quality of moral baseness or moral necessity;
and that, in consequence, such an act is either forbidden or enjoined by the author of nature, God" [1].

With such a definition of the law of nature, Grotius
proceeded to utilize it in regulating war. A further
passage is pertinent:

> Let the laws be silent, then, in the midst of arms, but
> only the laws of the State, those that the courts are
> concerned with, that are adapted only to the state of
> peace, not only those other laws, which are of perpetual
> validity and suited to all times, It was exceedingly well
> said by Dio of Prusa, that between enemies written laws
> that is, laws of particular states, are not in force, but that
> unwritten laws are in force that is, those which nature
> prescribes, or the agreement of nations has established [2].

Grotius believed that the law of nature is binding
upon states in their relations with each other. War,
however, is not in conflict with the law of nature. The
law of nations (*jus gentium*) also does not prevent the
justifiability of war. Grotius defined war as a condition

---

[1] *De Jure Belli ac Pacis* (Oxford: Clarendon Press, 1925), II, 38.
[2] *Ibid.*, p. 19.

of those contending by force, not as Cicero did as a contention by force [1].

On the question of the distinction between peoples with respect to war, Grotius makes some interesting comments. He states that a public war according to the law of nations is waged only between states. He quotes the definitions of war as given by the Roman jurists [2]. If a people are not composed into a state when they wage war, they are brigands and robbers [3]. "Grotius", as one student writes, "extended his rule to all nations and tribes of the earth, not discriminating between orientals and occidentals, coloured men and white men, uncivilized people and civilized people, non-Christians and Christians, non-Europeans and Europeans" [4]. He rebukes the Greeks for their contempt of the barbarians [5].

Aside from the qualification that a war is to be public or lawful according to the law of nations, it must be commenced by the sovereign [6] and waged between states. Grotius says that it must be publicly declared [7]. The obligation for a public declaration of war in order that it be a lawful war is based on the law

---

[1] *Ibid.*, p. 33.　　[2] *Ibid.*, p. 630.　　[3] *Ibid.*

[4] Van Vollenhoven, "Grotius and Geneva", *op. cit.*, p. 14.

[5] Grotius, *op. cit.*, p. 550.

[6] *Ibid.*, p. 102: "That power is called sovereign whose actions are not subject to the legal control of another, so that they cannot be rendered void by the operation of another human will". For a discussion of the ideas of Grotius on sovereignty, cf. Merriam, *op. cit.*, pp. 21–24.

[7] *Ibid.*, p. 633: "It is also necessary as we have said, that it should be publicly declared, and in fact proclaimed so publicly that the notification of this declaration be made by one of the parties to the other".

of nature and the law of nations. In some cases a declaration of war is not required by the law of nature. These are instances "where either an attack is being warded off, or a penalty is demanded from the very person who has done the wrong" [1]. A declaration of war is required, however, in all cases by the law of nations [2]. There are two kinds of declarations of war — conditional and absolute. It is in a case where the declaration is joined with a demand for restitution that the declaration is conditional [3]. When it is un-accompanied by any demands, it is absolute [4]. A declaration is necessary in order to show that the war is "being waged not by private initiative but by the will of each of the two peoples or their heads" [5]. It can be seen then that Grotius believed that a declaration of war was not always necessary according to the law of nature, but mandatory under the law of nations. A point worth mentioning is that he wrote that no interval of time is required between the declaration and commencement of hostilities, even though the practice of the Romans was contrary [6].

On the problem of the just war and the just cause of war Grotius makes an interesting distinction. A war that has been formally declared is legal according to the law of nations; a war that has not been formally declared is not necessarily illegal [7]. The wars which are not formally declared, "the law of nations does not indeed lend them support but it does not oppose

---

[1] *Ibid.*, p. 634.   [2] *Ibid.*   [3] *Ibid.*, p. 637.
[4] *Ibid.*, p. 638.   [5] *Ibid.*, p. 639.
[6] *Ibid.*, p. 640.   [7] *Ibid.*, p. 57.

them" [1]. It is apparent from this quotation that a war is legal according to the law of nations if it is formally declared. But a war that is not formally declared is not an illegal war, provided that it has a just cause. In other words, every war that is formally declared is legal in the law of nations, and every war that has a just cause is legal in the law of nature. The proposition is substantiated by Grotius' idea of the law of nature. Here is evident the notion that the law of nature transcends the law of nations. It should be pointed out, however, that Grotius does not face the question of whether or not a war is legal if it is properly declared, but with an unjust cause. There are three just causes of war — defense of self, recovery of property, and inflicting of punishment [2]. The basis for all just causes of war is an injury received [3]. It is worth mentioning that this was given by Cicero, and most of the churchmen and legists. In these categories, Grotius implies a justification for offensive war as well as defensive war which is explicitly affirmed. Grotius makes two exceptions to the justice of defensive war. One is in the case of the defense being solely undertaken to weaken the neighbor [4]; the other is in the situation where the defensive war is being waged by a prince who has given another country the just cause of war [5].

In considering the subject of unjust causes of war, Grotius first makes the distinction between un-justifiable and persuasive causes of war [6]. The latter

---

[1] *Ibid.*   [2] *Ibid.*, p. 171.   [3] *Ibid.*, p. 170.
[4] *Ibid.*, p. 184.   [5] *Ibid.*, p. 185.   [6] *Ibid.*, p. 546.

are only pretexts, while the former are the real causes. Wars which lack causes of either kind are wars of savages; wars that have only pretexts are wars of robbers [1]. Among the unjust causes of war, Grotius lists such things as: desire for richer lands, discovery of land belonging to others, desire for freedom among a subject people, and desire to rule others against their will on the pretext that it is for their own good [2].

On the question of whether a wrong intention with a just cause of war makes the war unlawful, Grotius says that it does not [3]. Like the various writers who preceded him, Grotius was concerned with the problem of the justice of war on both sides. He analyses the word "just" to mean either the deed or the doer. The doer can act justly "so long as he does not act unjustly, even if that which he does is not just" [4]. Now in reference to the deed, that is, the just cause of war, "a war cannot be just on both sides, as a legal claim cannot" [5]. Grotius continues,

> .... yet it may actually happen that neither of the warring parties does wrong. No one acts unjustly without knowing that he is doing an unjust thing, but in this respect many are ignorant. Thus either party may justly, that is in good faith, plead his case [6].

Most specifically he states, ".... if we interpret the word 'just' in relation to certain legal effects in this sense surely it may be admitted that a war may be just from the point of view of either side" [7].

---

[1] *Ibid.*, p. 547.   [2] *Ibid.*, pp. 550–1.
[3] *Ibid.*, p. 556.   [4] *Ibid.*, p. 565.   [5] *Ibid.*
[6] *Ibid.*   [7] *Ibid.*, p. 566.

From these quotations it seems self-evident that Grotius believed in the notion of "invincible ignorance" which made impossible the possession of a just cause of war only on one side. He added something to the controversy by holding that a war is just according to the law of nations not so much from the justice of its cause, because that is too difficult to discover but from the legality of its form — its declaration.

Grotius differed from Victoria and Suarez in that he pointed out the impossibility of an objective standard for justice. War was just according to its procedure. He gives the right of war a legal basis. Under his system he allows the state to carry on war measures to avoid some threatening danger. This implies a regard for the reason of State. It was the state's interest that was paramount.

The idea of the territorial sovereignty of states which was so emphasized by Grotius, is consistent with the high estimation for neutrality which he had. On the duty of neutrals towards belligerents, Grotius writes:

> On the other hand it is the duty of those who keep out of war to do nothing whereby he who supports a wicked cause may be rendered more powerful, or whereby the movements of him who wages a just war may be hampered, according to what we have said above. In a doubtful matter, however, those at peace should show themselves impartial to either side in permitting transit, in furnishing supplies to troops, and in not assisting those under siege [1].

Grotius seems to imply a kind of duty of a third state to help a state that is waging a just war. It may

---

[1] *Ibid.*, p. 786.

be recalled here that his definition of a just war is a rather broad one, in the sense that practically any cause can be made to be just. This point, therefore, is not too radical.

The present writer has failed to find in Grotius any limitations on war with respect to time and place.

A follower of both Gentili and Grotius was Richard Zouche (1589–1661) [1]. Not only was he, like his predecessor Gentili, a Regius Professor at Oxford, but also a judge of the English Admiralty court. His experience was an advantageous combination of theory and practice. The most renowned work of this writer is the *Juris et Judicii Feciales sine Juris inter Gentes, et Quaestionum de Eodem Explicatio* (1650). In this treatise he refers to what we call international law as *jus inter gentes* (law between peoples). This use of the Latin equivalent for the English term, international law, is most significant, for it shows that the notion of a law governing the relations of states was becoming more prominent. This was not the only innovation made by Zouche. Through his experiences as a lawyer and a judge of the Admiralty Court he regarded international law from a more positive viewpoint: that is, he resorted to treatises and the practices between states in making decisions. The use of positive practice of modern nations to form the law had appeared before in the work of Gentili, but it was not as marked as in

---

[1] Cf. Clark, *op. cit.*, pp. 127–128; Holdsworth, *op. cit.*, V, 17–18, 58–60; T. E. Holland, "Introduction" in Richard Zouche, *Juris et Judicii Feciales, Sine, Juris inter Gentes, et Quaestionum de Eodem Explicatio* (Washington: Carnegie Institution, 1911), I, i–ix.

the writings of Zouche. Zouche had a more extensive basis for his work than did Gentili because Grotius had already written his *De Jure Belli ac Pacis*. In this he had given to his age a definite position on the philosophic basis of international law. Zouche, then, was indebted to both Gentili and Grotius. A distinguished student of the history of English law has summed up the reasons for the significance of Zouche's work.

> In the first place, in his book international law appeared for the first time in a compact and orderly form. In the second place, he so clearly defined it that no one for the future could be under any misapprehension as to its scope. In the third place, he originated the modern division of the subject into Peace and War. In his book the tradition inherited from the medieaeval books of grouping the whole subject around the laws of War was finally abandoned [1].

Let us proceed with an analysis of the ideas of Zouche on the legal position of war. In the distinction between peoples with respect to war, Zouche makes some interesting comments. He writes as follows: "On the other hand it is averred that an attack can not justly be made on those who do not embrace the Christian religion" [2]. From this quotation it is apparent that Zouche did not recognize a distinction between Christians and infidels with respect to war.

The problem of the declaration of war concerned Zouche. With his method of studying the practice of the time, he discovered that in some cases a declaration of war was not given. This was demonstrated by

---

[1] Holdsworth, *op. cit.*, p. 59.

[2] *Juris et JudiciiFeciales, sine Juris inter Gentes et Quaestionum de Eodem Explicatio*, English translation by J. L. Brierly (Washington: Carnegie Institution, 1911), II, 116–117.

Gustavus Adolphus in his "defensive" war against Emperor Ferdinand the Second [1]. Zouche states that the law of nations does not "require an unjust attack made on a person to be repelled merely by heralds, when nature and the very circumstances allowed every man the use of arms for safety in such case" [2]. He pointed out that Gustavus Adolphus did not altogether omit a declaration of war, for he sent the Emperor notes demanding amends for the wrongs inflicted upon him [3]. There are certain cases, according to Zouche, in which a declaration of war may be sometimes "omitted for just cause; for instance: (1) when war is undertaken on the grounds of necessary defense; (2) when war is made on those who are already regarded as enemies; (3) when arms are taken up against rebels and deserters...." [4] and (4) when property is not returned or satisfaction is not given [5]. Zouche devotes a section to the question of whether or not war may be commenced at once after a declaration. He gives no answer, but merely states what some of his precursors held, among them Gentilis and Grotius [6]. The former believed that a thirty-three day period should elapse, and the latter held that no interval should be required after a declaration.

On the question of the just war, Zouche adds very little. A war is just in respect to the act or the person acting. In respect to the act, a war is just according to its cause; in respect to the person acting, a war is just if it is begun properly. This distinction is in Gentilis

---

[1] *Ibid.*, p. 171.   [2] *Ibid.*   [3] *Ibid.*   [4] *Ibid.*
[5] *Ibid.*, p. 172.   [6] *Ibid.*

and Grotius. Zouche takes up the question of whether
or not a war can be just on both sides [1]. He says that
in respect to the act itself, a war cannot be just on both
sides, but from the legality of the persons acting it can
be. The fact that the belligerents are acting under the
assumption that they are right makes the war just on
both sides [2]. It is interesting to note that Zouche
continues the doctrine of invincible ignorance. He
discusses the interpretation of the terms of truces, but
he gives no statement on the use of truces or limitations
of time to regulate war.

While Grotius set up a kind of dualism between the
law of nature and the law of nations, and Zouche
carried on this notion but gave preference to the law of
nations, that is, the branch of it which was positive, it
remained for Samuel von Pufendorf (1632–1694) to
reorient the problem of the relationship between natural law and international law [3]. Like Grotius he spent a
considerable part of his life in the employ of a foreign
monarch. A professor at the University of Lund in

[1] *Ibid.*, p. 112.
[2] *Ibid.*: "In respect of the act a war can not be just on both sides.
But it may well be that neither of the belligerents acts unjustly.
For none acts unjustly save he who knows that he is acting unjustly. Thus two persons may go to law justly, that is, in good faith,
on each side".
[3] Butler and Macoby, *op. cit.*, pp. 250–2; Dunning, *op. cit.*, pp.
318–25; Gettel, *op. cit.*, pp. 233–4; Hallam, *op. cit.*, II, 344–7;
Merriam, *op. cit.*, pp. 28–9; Walther Schücking, "Introduction"
in Samuel von Pufendorf, *De Officio Hominis et Avis Juxta Legem
Naturalem Libri Duo* (New York: Oxford University Press, 1927), II
9a–27a; Hans Wehberg, "Introduction" in Samuel von Pufendorf,
Elementorum Jurisprudentiae Universalis Libri Duo (Oxford: at the
Clarendon Press, 1931), II, xi–xxii; Westlake, *op. cit.*, pp. 63–65.

Sweden and later state historian at Stockholm, Pufendorf was personally an internationalist. Beginning his academic career in the field of theology, he went later into law and politics. It was Pufendorf who combined the political theory of the absolutists, who believed that there was no control over the actions of the state, with the theory of the internationalists like Grotius and Zouche. In his most famous work, the *De Jure Naturae et Gentium* (1672) he presents the epitome of the natural law philosophy as applied to human actions. This treatise was preceded by another work, his *Elementarum, Jurisprudentiae Universalis Libri Duo* (1660) [1]. Pufendorf regarded the law of nations as a part of natural law; he writes as follows: "Something must be added now also on the subject of the Law of Nations, which, in the eyes of some men, is nothing other than the law of nature in so far as different nations, not united with another by a supreme command, observe it, who must render one another the same duties in their fashion as are prescribed for individuals by the law of nature" [2].

On the question of the distinction between peoples with respect to war, Pufendorf held that the fact that the American Indians were savages and barbarians, did not give a nation the right to wage war upon them [3].

---

[1] Samuel von Pufendorf, *Elementorum Jurisprudentiae Universalis Libri Duo*. English translation by W. A. Oldfather (Oxford: Clarendon Press, 1931), Vol. II.

[2] *Ibid.*, p. 165.

[3] *Of the Law of Nature and Nations*, Translated by Basil Kennett (London: J. Walthoe *et al*, 1729), p. 837.

The problem of the declaration of war concerned Pufendorf. He wrote:

> External war is war between those who are not comprised in the same state. This is wont to be divided into *formal* and *less formal*. The former is also called a regular war according to the law of nations (by that meaning of the word regular whereby a regular army is opposed to some irregular troop of bandits) and is a war carried on by the highest power in the state, following a declaration. The purpose of this declaration is not that the enemy may have time to prepare himself for resistance but to make clear that the war is not being conducted as the private venture of a few, but as a public enterprise, and that the enemy may accordingly know with whom he will have to deal. As for the rest, wars that are destitute of such requisites are less formal. But when others are attacked in secret raids and by an irregular band, upon no public authority, without declaration, and without first cause, this is called freebooting [1].

The clearness of this passage quoted above compensates for the large space given to it. Pufendorf regards war as a legal institution. He implied that in order for it to be so it must be between states which are sovereign. The highest authority in the state must assent to the war. A declaration must precede hostilities, and the war must have a just cause. If all these conditions are not present, it is not a war in the legal sense, that is, according to the law of nations.

What were the just causes of war according to Pufendorf? They are of three kinds: (1) to defend persons and properties, (2) to assert rights that have been ignored, and (3) to recover satisfaction for damages or a guarantee for the future [2]. The first cause of war is

---

[1] *Elementorum Jurisprudentiae*, II, 13–14.
[2] *Ibid.*, p. 834. *De Officio Hominis et Civis Juxta Legem Naturalem*

defensive, while the second and third are offensive [1]. It is obvious that a war can be both just and offensive. As for the unjust causes of war, Pufendorf follows those laid down by Grotius. They are avarice, ambition, fears arising from the strength and power of neighbors, and utility [2].

Pufendorf takes up the problem of doubt arising over a just cause of war. This is particularly true in cases of offensive war [3]. When through ignorance or negligence, cases of doubt arise, the dispute should be attempted to be settled by mediation, arbitration, or lot [4]. When there is no doubt as to whether the cause is just, resort should be made to arbitration, in order to establish the justice or injustice of the cause [5]. According to Pufendorf whoever commences a war without first submitting the dispute to a "pacific settlement" does not have a just cause of war, for if a state goes to war without doing this, it waives all rights it has to possessing a just cause [6]. What is very interesting in the idea is that it was very similar to that advanced by William Jennings Bryan, when he was Secretary of State. This point is given further support by Pufendorf. He says that if a state has offered an amicable settlement of the dispute, and this means is rejected, and if the unjust aggressor conquers

---

Libri Duo, English translation by F. G. Moore (New York: Oxford Univ. Press, 1927), II, 138.

[1] *Ibid.*

[2] *Of the Law of Nature and Nations*, pp. 836–37.

[3] *Ibid.*, p. 835.   [4] *Ibid.*   [5] *Ibid.*, pp. 554–55.

[6] *Elementorum Jurisprudentiae*, II, 145.

the state, the state is not bound by the peace treaty [1]. In other words, this substantiates Pufendorf's point that, in order to have a just cause of war, one must submit the dispute first to an amicable settlement, and if this is refused he implied that the enemy is an unjust aggressor.

As for neutrality and the duty of third states to go to war, Pufendorf is not very specific. He implies neutrality and, of course, under his system of natural law, all states are bound to obey it. Peace is in keeping with natural law, but war is necessary in some cases and is not in violation of natural law [2].

Pufendorf's system is more philosophical than legal. He is vague in his discussion of the concrete problems of international law. Some mention is made of a time limitation on war, the temporary suspension of hostilities-truces [3]. They are, however, for such things as the burial of the dead. He notes also the practice of immunizing places from warfare.

Under the system of natural law the existence of a positive international law was denied by Pufendorf. He wrote that states are subject only to the law of nature. There were usages of nations such as customs and treaties, but they could be renounced at any time. Such a system was inconsistent. It was also weak in that it presented no definite basis for international law except the law of nature.

A contemporary of Pufendorf, Samuel Rachel

---

[1] *Of the Law of Nature and Nations*, p. 854.
[2] *Elementorum*, p. 96.
[3] *Ibid.*

(1628–1691) [1] demonstrated that besides the law of nature there was a positive law of nations. Like Pufendorf, he was German born, began his academic training in theology, and later changed to jurisprudence. During part of his life he was professor of the Law of Nature and International Law at the University of Kiel.

Rachel's outstanding work is the *De Jure Naturae et Gentium Dissertationes* (1676). He regarded the law of nations as a form of "arbitrary law" which is based on agreements or custom [2]. He defines the law of nations as follows: "The Law of Nations then, is a law developed by the consent or agreement either expressly or tacitly given, of many free nations whereby for the sake of utility they are mutually bound to one another" [3]. Rachel does not deny the existence of the law of nature; he merely allocates it to a particular sphere. In other words he does not entirely dispense with the law of nature, but he extends and restricts paradoxically enough the limits of the law of nations. He says that there is a law of nations other than the law of nature [4]. As he writes:

.... the whole of the Law of Nations has been developed and established for reasons of Utility, this will perhaps remain unchallenged, and I shall have succeeded in convincing every one that all Arbitrary Law has this end and that the Law of Nations is one branch thereof. Under Utility, I include Necessity, for the more necessary anything is to us the more need we have of it as a useful thing [5].

[1] Cf. Samuel Rachel, *De Jure Naturae et Gentium Dissertationes*, "Introduction" by Ludwig von Bar, English translation by J. P. Bate (Washington, D. C.: Carnegie Institution, 1916), II, 7a–16a.
[2] *Ibid.*, p. 163.   [3] *Ibid.*, p. 170.   [4] Cf. *Ibid.*, p. 181.
[5] *Ibid.*, pp. 182–3.

On the problem of the legality of war, these general principles are evident. Rachel says that there are two kinds of law, natural and arbitrary, and that both exercise their authority over war [1]. He holds that some wars are just according to his theory. If a war is "lawful from the standpoint of the Law of Nations, in regard of the manner of its commencement, it must be undertaken on the authority and under the auspices of him who has Sovereignty, in the State" [2]. He uses the word "just" in the Roman sense of a just will or a just marriage, that is, just in the procedural sense. He adds:

> Even this is not enough to make a war just according to the Law of Nations. It is so only when it is publicly ordained by the Sovereign in such a way that it is signified to the other party solemnly or in the accepted fashion, as by solemn Promulgation, Declaration, Denunciation, or Heraldic Proclamation [3].

A war then according to Rachel is just according to the law of nations if it is declared by the sovereign, and made public so that the enemy will know of it. If a war is just according to the law of nature, it must (1) have a just cause, (2) be necessary, and (3) have the objective of peace [4]. By a just cause, Rachel means "some hurt that has been done wrongfully to one of your interests" [5]. Such a hurt must be sufficiently serious [6]. He defines necessity as the impossibility of obtaining satisfaction through offering reparation; or through any other peaceful means [7]. Even if a war

---

[1] *Ibid.*, p. 183.   [2] *Ibid.*, pp. 184–5.   [3] *Ibid.*, p. 185.
[4] Cf. *ibid.*, pp. 183–4.   [5] *Ibid.*, p. 183.   [6] *Ibid.*
[7] *Ibid.*, pp. 183–4.

has a just cause and is necessary, it should not be resorted to except when peace is the end [1]. This distinction between a war which is just according to the law of nations and just according to the law of nature is interesting. It shows that Rachel had in mind a distinction, let us say, between international ethics and international law. It is worth adding here that Rachel made war legal according to the law of nations by its authoritative declaration. He emphasizes the point when he said that even if the other side has a just cause, "the infliction of injury and damage by each side on the other is lawful" [2].

It is obvious that under Rachel's system there was no duty of third states to go to war. He does mention truces [3] which are examples of time limitations on war.

A contemporary of Rachel was his fellow countryman, Johann Wolfgang Textor (1638–1701) [4]. Like Pufendorf and Rachel, he was a German professor who had studied theology and jurisprudence. His outstanding work in international law is the *Synopsis Juris Gentium* (1680). Like Rachel, Textor believed in the dual existence of the law of nature and the law of nations. He did not, as Rachel did, draw such a sharp distinction between the two. His conception of the law of nations was that usage and reason composed it [5]. The law of nations was not strictly positive, but it had also an element of natural law in it. Textor, however,

---

[1] *Ibid.*, p. 184.   [2] *Ibid.*, p. 185.   [3] *Ibid.*, p. 188.
[4] Cf. Johann Wolfgang Textor, *Synopsis Juris Gentium*, "Introduction" by Ludwig von Bar, English translation by J. P. Bate (Washington: Carnegie Institution, 1916), II, 7a–26a.
[5] *Ibid.*, p. 1.

failed to make clear which was to prevail when there was a conflict between usage and reason.

On the distinction between peoples with respect to war, Textor made specific comments. He held that war could not be justly made "on Mohametan peoples or pagans and barbarians because of defects in their religion" [1]. This he substantiated by saying that non-belief is not in itself an injury to believers [2]. It is worth noting that Textor did believe that some of the Crusades were unjustified [3].

Textor defines war as "a condition of lawful hostile offense existing for just cause between royal or quasi-royal powers, declared by public authority" [4]. This definition includes three things, the war must be between sovereigns; it must be declared by public authority; and it must have a just cause. Although the declaration of war is still necessary according to Textor, the solemnities for declaring it have fallen into disuse [5]. He says that it is discretionary whether the war be declared by ambassadors or otherwise, as by a written proclamation [6].

Just causes of war resolve themselves into two general categories (1) "a serious grievance suffered by the party making the war; (2) a refusal of redress by the other side" [7]. Should the other side offer to redress the grievance, then there is no justice to the cause of war [8]. He divides the causes of war into two groups — "justificatory" and "persuasive" [9]. The former are

---

[1] *Ibid.*, p. 176.   [2] *Ibid.*   [3] Cf. *ibid.*, pp. 179–80.
[4] *Ibid.*, p. 160.   [5] *Ibid.*, p. 181.   [6] *Ibid.*
[7] *Ibid.*, p. 167.   [8] *Ibid.*, p. 168.   [9] *Ibid.*, p. 169.

those which make war just either according to the law
of nations or to the intent of the belligerent [1]. The
latter is the use of arms for expediency [2]. A war is not
just from the standpoint of the law of nations unless the
cause, whether it be the real one, the justificatory one,
or a pretext, is "adequately relevant and just" [3].
Textor emphasized the necessity of distinguishing the
real causes from the justificatory causes and pretexts.
He accuses Grotius of failing to do this. There are
three just causes of an offensive war. These are "injuries to the body, to the reputation, and to property" [4].
He takes up specific questions as the refusal of passage
of troops which he shows are not in some conditions
just causes of war [5]. There are just and unjust causes
of defensive war. If an attack is made because the
person attacked has not complied with the demand for
satisfaction, then the defense is not justifiable [6]. The
injustice does not lie in repelling force by force, but
in the defense's refusal of a just redress [7]. When the
offensive war, of course, is unjust, the defensive war is
just. He summarizes as follows: "In sum, whenever the
cause of war is obviously just on the side of the aggressor, as when some overwhelming loss had notori-
ously been caused by the other side and no fitting
recompense has been given on demand then there is no
just cause in the defensive war" [8].

Textor considers the question of whether a war can
be just on both sides. He follows the notion of Molina.

---

[1] *Ibid.*, p. 169.   [2] *Ibid.*   [3] *Ibid.*, p. 170.
[4] *Ibid.*   [5] *Ibid.*, p. 178.   [6] *Ibid.*, p. 180.
[7] *Ibid.*   [8] *Ibid.*, p. 181.

This allows for justice of a war even in case there is doubt as to its cause. There must be, however, some inquiry into the nature of the doubtful cause, if the war is to be just [1]. It is not necessary to have a just cause in the material sense, in order to require a just war. Only an "adequately relevant and just cause" is demanded. Textor admits "that under the Law of Nations, there are degrees in the justice of causes of war" [2]. This whole argument is embedded with the theory of probabilism as worked out by Molina.

Textor enumerates three grades of distinction in the causes of war [3]. The first are those depending on the mere beliefs of the authors of war without any regard to the probability of the relevancy of the cause. The second are those depending on the beliefs of the authors of the war, not manifestly improbably, but accompanied by just ignorance of the greater probabilities on the other side. The third are those depending "not only in the belief of the author of the war, but also in the fact that the cause itself is, in itself and absolutely speaking, more just and more probable" [4]. The first are inadequate causes, but the second and third are adequate when they are at their best. Although Textor states that it is impossible for a war to have material justice on both sides [5], he holds that material justice is not necessary for a just war. It is not the justice of the cause, per se, because this is difficult to ascertain, but the justice of the cause as believed by the author of the war, that determines the

---

[1] *Ibid.*, pp. 174–5. [2] *Ibid.*, p. 175. [3] *Ibid.*, pp. 175–6.
[4] *Ibid.*, p. 176. [5] Cf. *Ibid.*, p. 174.

justice of the war. In accordance with this point of view, a war can be just on both sides from the standpoint of the law of nations. Like so many writers, Textor says as follows: "Of course, every effort ought to be made to settle the dispute of Kings and peoples by some other method than arms; for instance, in a friendly way through diplomacy, or perhaps by a kind of compromise in accordance with the decision of skilled arbiters" [1].

Textor comprehended neutrality in the sense of a state being neither an ally nor a friend to the belligerents [2]. Neutrality according to the usage of the law of nations is a condition that emanates from consent or agreement. His definition is: "Neutrality, then, is simply the right of equal friendship with each or all of the belligerent parties, constituted by consent or agreement" [3]. It is necessary for the belligerents to consent to the neutrality, and of course, a belligerent who does not give his consent, is not bound to recognize the neutrality of a third state [4]. This consent, however, can be given tacitly [5]. With respect to the idea that there is a duty of third states to go to war in the case where a recalcitrant state refuses to keep the peace, Textor makes to specific comment. He does say, however, that a party may be compelled to quit the state of neutrality [6]. This means apparently, although he does not specifically say so, that neutrality exists by consent and even if a third state may want to be

---

[1] *Ibid.*, p. 176.   [2] *Ibid.*, p. 273.   [3] *Ibid.*

[4] *Ibid.*, p. 274.   [5] *Ibid.*, p. 278.   [6] *Ibid.*, p. 276.

neutral, the state is not neutral, if either belligerent does not desire it to remain neutral.

Textor discusses the neutralization of certain territories[1]. This, of course, is a limitation on war with respect to place. He applies also the word "truce" to include this limitation of war in provinces and towns for an indefinite period [2]. The restrictions on war as to time are either truces for an unlimited period, or for a definite duration [3].

Summary. — In the seventeenth century the theory and practice of the legality of war assumed a less rigid and less definite form. The system of the balance of power, which had been developed in an attempt to maintain peace, had been challenged by the Thirty Years' War but as a result had been made more permanent. The distinction between peoples with respect to war was scarcely made either in the theory or the practice of the time. Grotius, who was greatly influenced by the Thirty Years' War, wrote that a public war was fought only between states, but aside from this he made no distinction between peoples as to war. Zouche made a positive statement that there was no difference between Christians and infidels with reference to war. Pufendorf approached the problem by using the American Indians as an example. He said that the fact that the Indians were savages and barbarians did not give a nation the right to go to war on them. Rachel seemed to have made no reference to this problem. Textor, discussing it from the standpoint of the Mohammetans, wrote that because they were

---

[1] *Ibid.*, p. 275.   [2] *Ibid.*, p. 208.   [3] Cf. *ibid.*, pp. 207–215.

pagans, there was no general right to wage war on them. It is clear then that none of the principal writers on international law during the seventeenth century made a general distinction between peoples with respect to war.

On the question of the declaration of war, both practice and theory were more definite. With the introduction of the use of printed papers, there developed the practice of sending a printed declaration of war, a custom which in turn disappeared when permanent embassies were established. Not all wars in the seventeenth century, however, were preceded by a declaration. In a few instances the formality was not observed. All of the leading writers on international law were concerned with the problem of the declaration of war during the seventeenth century. Grotius, for instance, held that a war must be declared publicly. He even went so far as to say that the law of nations always requires a public declaration. There were, according to him, two kinds of declarations, absolute, that is, when no demand was made, and conditional, that is, when the declaration was accompanied by a demand for restitution. Zouche, a more positive writer on international law than Grotius, observed that not all wars were opened by a declaration. It is interesting to note that Zouche, believing that the law of nations did not always require a declaration of war, made some exceptions to the Grotian rule, as in the case of necessary defense. Pufendorf, on the other hand maintained that a legal war should be preceded by a declaration. A just war according to the law of nations in the words of Rachel, was one that was declared by the sovereign. Textor also stated that a declaration was required. It should be noted that of all these writers, the most positive one, Zouche, did not always require a declaration of war.

The question of the just war and the just cause of war had begun to decline in importance by the seventeenth century. Grotius gave to war a legal basis, but by making the law of nations coincide with the law of nature, he kept some of the moralistic notions of war. His main idea was that the causes of war had a legal significance and that they should be considered in such a manner. A just war was one which was in defense of law; an unjust war one which was in opposition to law. There were three just causes of war: defense of self, recovery of property, and inflicting of punishment. Grotius allowed a state to carry on war measures in order to avoid some threatening danger. He even employed the idea of the reason of state. He thus marked the transition between the mediaeval theory of the just war and the succeeding centuries' notion of the reason of state as a just basis of war.

Zouche added very little to the notion of the just war. Although he followed the Grotian categories of the just and unjust causes of war, Pufendorf made an interesting contribution. He said that, in order to have a just cause of war, a state should first submit the dispute to a "pacific settlement". Rachel made a novel distinction on the subject of just war. According to him a just war under the law of nations was not required to have a just cause, but a just war according to the law of nature had to possess this requisite. His conception of a just cause was a wrong received. Textor made no such careful distinction; he merely enumerated the just causes of war, at the same time affirming that a war can have just causes on both sides.

During the seventeenth century the idea of neutrality was beginning to be fairly well formulated, but the notion of the duty of third states to go to war was not worked out. All of the leading writers, Grotius, Zouche, Pufendorf, Rachel, and Textor discussed neutrality. Only Grotius seemed to imply a duty of third states to help a state wage a just war. Of the limitations on war with respect to time, Rachel and Textor made some mention. Textor alone discussed some of the limitations on the place of waging war.

CHAPTER V

THE EIGHTEENTH CENTURY

Practice. — As was pointed out before, the European states' system was challenged by the political ambitions of Louis XIV in the seventeenth century. He continued to disturb the equilibrium of Europe even into the early part of the eighteenth century [1]. The War of the Spanish Succession which was waged for ten years was ended by the Peace of Utrecht in 1713. This marked the re-establishment of the balance of power idea which was not greatly disturbed until the French Revolution. Although the eighteenth century was an age of reason, yet it was also an age of despots, and more particularly in the concern of this study, an age of wars. From the War of the Spanish Succession to the French Revolution there were about twenty wars.

---

[1] Cf. for political background of the eighteenth century: *Cambridge Modern History*, Vol. VI (New York: Macmillan Co., 1909); Gettell, *op. cit.*, pp. 238–40, 278–80; Arthur Hasall, *Balance of Power, 1715–1789* (London: Rivington's, 1922); F. Meinecke, *Weltbürgertum und Nationalstaat* (5th ed.; München und Berlin: Druck und Verlag von R. Oldenbourg, 1919); R. B. Mowat, *The Age of Reason* (Boston: Houghton Mifflin Co., 1934); Mowat, *European Diplomacy, 1451–1789*, pp. 154–300; Mowat, *European States System*, pp. 31–40; F. L. Schuman, *International Politics* (New York: McGraw–Hill Book Company, 1933), pp. 80–85; P. Smith, *History of Modern Culture*, II, 3–16.

During the eighteenth century there was still the problem of distinguishing peoples with respect to war. This was evident in the wars of the French and the British against the Indians in the New World, and also in the British wars in India. On the question of the declaration of war, the practice of the eighteenth century was to begin a war without a formal declaration [1]. It has been estimated that between 1700 and 1871 in only ten wars were there declarations [2]. Some of these were: the War of the Spanish Succession, the Seven Years' War, and the English war against the French in 1778 [3].

There seems to have been very little concern in practice over the just war and just causes of war in the eighteenth century. International law was regarded mostly as a set of usages for diplomats and rules for royal succession. It was with respect to neutrality, more particularly, the neutral rights at sea that the development in international law really came. Since practically every European state had been more or less directly involved in the frequent wars of the period, a weak power was in an unfortunate situation if it wanted to demand its neutral rights. To take care of this predicament there were organized in the eighteenth century, leagues of states for the realization of neutrality. In 1693 Denmark and Sweden had formed a league to demand their neutral rights when England and Spain were combatting France. This was one of

---

[1] Holland, *Lectures*, p. 253.
[2] *Ibid.*
[3] *Ibid.*, p. 254.

the many precedents which paved the way for the
Armed Neutrality of Russia, Sweden, and Denmark of
1780, which later drew in Holland, Prussia, Austria,
Portugal, and Naples [1].

The eighteenth century practice then showed little
regard for the legal status of war. The foreign policy
of the states paid scarcely any attention to whatever
natural law which was regarded as underlying the rules
for beginning war. It can be said that the eighteenth
century was a period which saw the decadence of the
attempts to regulate war effectively through international law.

International Law Writers. — The outstanding
positive international law writer during the early
eighteenth century was Cornelius van Bynkershoek
(1673–1743) [2]. His life was spent mostly in the service
of his native country, the Netherlands. From his early
interest in Roman law, he later turned to international
law. It was his experience as a judge in the Supreme
Court of Holland, Zealand, and Western Frisia that
gave him the unique opportunity to consider the
various problems of the law of nations. His most
important work is the *Quaestionum Juris Publici,*
published first in 1737 in a volume composed of two

---

[1] Cf. Butler and Maccoby, *op. cit.*, p. 233.

[2] Cf. J. de Louter, "Introduction" in C. van Bynkershoek,
Quaestionum Juris Publici Libri Duo (Oxford: Clarendon Press,
1930), II, ix–xlvi; James Brown Scott, "Introduction" in C. van
Bynkershoek, *De Dominio Maris Dissertatio* (New York: Oxford
University Press, 1923), pp. 13–22; John Westlake, *Collected Papers*
pp. 67–70.

books, the first of which treats war, the second, various
political and legal subjects. In this work he defines
war as "a contest of independent persons carried on by
force or fraud for the sake of asserting their rights" [1].
"Independent persons" applies not only to states but
also to "individuals not living in an organized state" [2].
Bynkershoek discards the distinction between public
and private war. He follows the Grotian conception of
war which is that war is a condition rather than an
action [3]. It is clear that he subscribes to the notion
that war can exist only between persons and states
which have no superior authority. The problem of the
status of a primitive people in time of war was
considered by Bynkershoek. He made no distinction
between the so-called Barbary peoples of Africa
and the European peoples with respect to war [4].
Pirates, he held, could be "punished by the forfeiture
of life and goods" [5]. Bynkershoek thus implies that
pirates are outside the realm of the law of war.

The problem of the declaration of war concerned
Bynkershoek. Although some demand for satisfaction
must be made for the "injuries sustained or complained
of", yet a war may be lawful without a formal declaration [6]. He differs from Grotius who held that the law

---

[1] C. van Bynkershoek, *Quaestionum Juris Publici Libri Duo*,
English translation by Tenney Frank (Oxford: Clarendon Press,
1930), II, 15.
[2] *Ibid.*
[3] Cf. J. de Louter, "Introduction", *op. cit.*, p. xiii.
[4] Cf. *Quaestionum*, II, 98 ff.
[5] *Ibid.*, p. 98.
[6] *Ibid.*, p. 18.

of nations required a formal declaration [1]. He held that "the dictates of reason, whose authority is so great in defining the law of nations" does not require a formal declaration of war [2]. "If two sovereigns are engaged in hostilities without having declared war, can we have any doubt that war is being waged according to the will of both?" [3] Not only reason, but also current practice supported this point, according to Bynkershoek. The war between Spain and the United Provinces, the invasion of Germany by Gustavus Adolphus, and the war between Louis XIV and Spain were all begun without formal declarations [4]. The inference is that all of these wars were not illegal in so far as they had no formal declaration.

On the question of the just war, Bynkershoek makes no specific reference. In his definition of war, he says that the end of war is the maintenance of rights. An exponent of Bynkershoek, J. de Louter, finds in this definition the implication of the just cause of war [5]. The present writer, however, finds no elucidation of this implication in Bynkershoek's writings.

Being a Dutchman, it is of no mean significance that he worked out such clear notions of neutrality. Neutrals are those "who belong to neither belligerent party and who owe no services to either party by treaty

---

[1] Cf. Butler and Maccoby, *op. cit.*, p. 194. These writers make the error in saying that Bynkershoek agreed with Grotius in requiring a declaration of war.

[2] *Ibid.*, pp. 20–21.

[3] *Ibid.*, p. 21.

[4] *Ibid.*, pp. 21–25.

[5] Cf. J. de Louter, "Introduction", *op. cit.*, p. xiii.

obligations" [1]. His main source for recognizing the
practice of neutrality was custom. Bynkershoek's
statement of the position of a neutral against a so-
called just belligerent marks a distinct change [2]. He
wrote:

> If I do not deceive myself, the justice or injustice of the
> war does not affect a common friend. It is not for him to
> place himself as a judge between the two belligerents who
> are the one and the other, his friends; nor, on the ground
> that their cause is the more just or less, accord or refuse
> more or less to this one or that. If I am neither on one side
> or the other, I can not aid the one in such a way as will
> hurt the other [3].

In another instance, he virtually restates this position: "In my judgment the question of justice and
injustice does not concern the neutral, and it is not
his duty to sit in judgment between his friends who
may be fighting each other, and to grant or deny anything to either belligerent through considerations of
the relative degree of justice" [4].

Another well known positive writer on international
law during the eighteenth century was the German,
Johann Jacob Moser (1701–1785) [5]. Educated at the
University of Tübingen, where he eventually became a
professor, Moser spent the most important part of his
life as a district counselor in Württemburg. An author
of many volumes, Moser is famous as an early German
systematizer of international law.

[1] *Quaestionum*, II, 60.
[2] Cf. Butler and Maccoby, *op. cit.*, p. 232.
[3] Quoted in Butler and Maccoby, *op. cit.*, p. 232.
[4] *Quaestionum*, p. 61.
[5] Cf. *Encyclopaedia Britannica*, XV (1919), 842.

His greatest work is the *Versuch des neuesten Europäischen Völkerrechts in Friedens- und Kriegs-Zeiten*
(1777–1780). As to the declaration of war, he says that
international law requires a public declaration before
or at the beginning of hostilities [1]. It is only the sovereign who can declare war [2]. After the sovereign has
issued a declaration of war, it is required that the other
party give a counter declaration [3]. Accompanying
these declarations the reasons for war are stated [4].
Although Moser does not seem to directly refer to the
idea of just causes of war, he lays down two "war
reasons". The first is that the existing conditions make
the war necessary, and the second is that the current
custom of European states has justified war under
those circumstances [5]. Moser defines neutrality as
that condition in which a sovereign shows impartiality
toward both belligerents [6].

   While Bynkershoek was the most outstanding writer
of the positive school of international law during the

---

[1] Moser, *Versuch des neuesten Europäischen Völkerrechts* (Frankfort am Main: Varrentropp Sohn und Wenner, 1779), IX, 30: "Es
ist Völkerrechtens, dass, wann ein Staat den andern mit Krieg
überziehen will solches vor oder bei Anfang derer Feindseligkeiten
öffentlich Völkerrechts".

[2] Cf. *ibid.*, IX, 36.

[3] *Ibid.*, IX, 37: "Auf eine Kriegserklärung pfleget sodann der
andere Theil eine Gegen-Kriegserklärung herauszugeben".

[4] Cf. *ibid.*, IX, 37–38.

[5] *Ibid.*, IX, 115: "Der Grund des Kriegsraison bestehet also
darinn: 1. Dass die vorliegende Umstande es nöthig machen und 2.
dass andere Europäische Staaten in anderen ähnlichen Fällen der-
gleichen auch für erlaubt gehalten haben".

[6] *Ibid.*, X, 148: "Neutralität ist wann ein Souverain gegen den
Kriegsführenden Theilen sich unparthenisch erzeiget".

early part of the eighteenth century, and Moser of the same school during the middle of the same century, George Friedrich de Martens (1756–1808) [1] was probably the most widely known positivist during the latter part of that century. Aside from being a compiler of treatises, Professor de Martens wrote a rather extensive statement of international law, *Précis du Droit des Gens Moderne de l'Europe* (1789) [2]. War is defined as "that state, in which men constantly exercise acts of indeterminent violence against each other" [3]. It is evident that he recognized, as did Bynkershoek, that war is a condition. He classified war in the categories of public and private. The first exists between individuals in a state of nature, the second, between men in society [4]. Public war is of two kinds, civil and national [5]. War in the sense of international law is national war. "National war is a conflict between nation and nation. It never can be undertaken or carried on by the authority of the sovereign...." [6].

As to the declaration of war, he says: "The universal law of nations acknowledges no general obligation of making a declaration of war to the enemy, previous to the commencement of hostilities" [7]. He wrote further: "Many of the ancient nations looked on such

---

[1] Cf. Robert Figge, *Georg Friedrich von Martens Sein Leben und seine Werke*, Inaugural-Dissertation (Gleiwiss: P. Hill's Buchdruckerei, 1914); Gilbert Gidel, "Droit et Devoirs des Nations", *Hague. Académie de Droit International. Recueil des Cours* (Paris: librairie Hachette, 1927), X, 585–89.

[2] *Summary of the Law of Nations*, English translation by William Cobbett (Philadelphia: Thomas Bradford, 1795).

[3] *Ibid.*, p. 271.   [4] *Ibid.*   [5] *Ibid.*

[6] *Ibid.*, p. 272.   [7] *Ibid.*, p. 274.

a declaration as essential and it was practiced in Europe, till the seventeenth century; but now-a-days nations content themselves with publishing a declaration of war through their own dominions and explaining their motives to other powers in writing" [1].

Before we present his ideas on the just causes of war, it is necessary to note a further distinction which de Martens draws between offensive and defensive national wars [2]. Normally speaking, the former he regards as referring to a war where the first act of violence is begun by a sovereign. The sovereign who receives this first act of violence in so doing makes the war a defensive one [3]. If a sovereign foresees an attack, he may take up arms in order to protect himself. He is thus waging a defensive war and not an offensive one [4]. While de Martens seems to imply that only a defensive war is justified, he works out no precise formula to determine the nature of such a war. In general he does say, however, that either the reception of an act of violence or the anticipation of one would justify a defensive war. As he wrote: "Nothing short of the violation of a perfect right either committed or with which a nation is threatened in the future can justify the undertaking of a war" [5]. De Martens does not mean to imply that the reception or the anticipation of an act of violence gives a nation a *carte blanche* to wage war. The injured party can resort to arms only "when amicable means have been tried in vain or when it is evident that it would be useless to try such

---

[1] *Ibid.*, pp. 274–5.   [2] *Ibid.*, p. 272.
[3] *Ibid.*, pp. 272–3.   [4] *Ibid.*, p. 273.   [5] *Ibid.*

means" [1]. This holds in all cases except where the belligerents have agreed by treaty that certain injuries shall not be regarded as sufficient grounds for war [2]. It is interesting to note that de Martens like so many of the early writers, especially the positivists who held that a war could be just on both sides, believed that the belligerents could think and act as though both sides were just [3].

On the notion of neutrality, de Martens is very specific. He wrote: "A state, not engaged to either of the belligerent powers by a treaty of alliance, or bound to them by the ties of vassalage, association, etc., is under no perfect obligation to take part in the war" [4]. It is obvious that he did not comprehend any duty of third states to go to war against a recalcitrant state. Nor does he discuss the question of the limitations on war in respect to time and place.

Outside of Grotius, the first important writer on international law to combine the natural law school with the positive school of jurisprudence was Christian Wolff (1679–1754) [5]. Born and educated in Germany,

---

[1] *Ibid.*, p. 273.

[2] Cf. *ibid.*, footnote.

[3] *Ibid.*, p. 274: "It is impossible that the sentiments of the belligerent parties should not be in direct opposition with regard to the justice or injustice of the war, yet if it be not manifoldly unjust, their own welfare induces them to consider it as lawful, as far as respects the treatment of the enemy and the validity of conventions and treaties of peace".

[4] *Ibid.*, p. 310.

[5] Cf. Gettel, *op. cit.*, p. 241; Gidel, "Droit et Devoirs des Nations" *op. cit.*, pp. 565–77; O. Nippold, "Introduction", in Christian Wolff's *Jus Gentium Methodo Scientifica Petractatum*, Trans. by Francis. J. Hemelt (Oxford: Clarendon Press, 1934), Vol. II;

he exemplifies the outstanding currents of thought which permeated his country. A very profound student with an interest in mathematics, astronomy, physics, philosophy, theology, and law, he was in great demand by the German universities. His renown extended beyond the borders of his native land. He was called to London, St. Petersburg, Paris, and Copenhagen.

His most famous work on international law is the *Jus Gentium Methodo Scientifica Pertractatum* (1754). A most prolific writer, Wolff produced a new work practically every year. The great range of subjects which interested him was manifested in the different kinds of books he wrote. His literary goal was to bring all knowledge together; his personal ambition was to be a teacher of the world. Both of these heights were almost realized. Although only a part of his life was spent in the study of international law, he, nevertheless, ranks as an important writer in this field of learning. His following was extensive. Probably if it had not been for Wolff's book, Vattel would not have written on international law.

As has been said above, Wolff's system of international law [1] comprised the mergence of his *jus gentium* with his *jus naturale*. This he called natural international law (*jus gentium naturale*). With this concept Wolff lays down his principle that nations have a set of rights

---

Christian Wolff, *Jus Gentium Methodo Scientifica Pertractatum*, Trans. by J. H. Drake (Oxford: Clarendon Press, 1934), Vol. II; J. Westlake, *Collected Papers*, pp. 70–76.

[1] Mention should be made of Thomasius (1655–1728) who differed from his contemporary, Wolff, in distinguishing natural law from positive law.

and duties toward each other, which arise from the immutable law of nature. In this relationship, all nations are equal.

Besides the natural international law, there is voluntary international law (*jus gentium voluntarium*). This is formed from the realization by nations that in order to safeguard their rights they must establish a society of nations which he calls the *Civitas Maxima*. From the nature of this society, there emanates a right of the *Civitas Maxima* over each nation. The law which is deduced from this concept of the society of nations is the voluntary international law. In addition to the natural international law and the voluntary international law, Wolff distinguishes also international treaty law and customary international law.

Wolff was concerned with many aspects of the problem of the legality of war. He wrote that controversies can be settled between nations. "Since controversies between nations can be settled in the same manner as those between private individuals living in a state of nature, and since by natural law they can be settled either amicably, or through compromise, or through mediation, or finally through arbitration or submission to arbiters, controversies between nations also can be settled either amicably or through compromise, or through mediation or arbitration" [1].

Wolff does not believe that this takes away the right of war. In his own words he says: "Since the right of war belongs to the nation offering a conference for an amicable adjustment, or compromise, or for a

---

[1] Wolff, *op. cit.*, p. 290.

submission to arbiters, against the nation unwilling to accept, so that the nation may be driven to settlement by force of arms, and since it is just the same whether the refusal is express or tacit, if it can be easily foreseen that a conference or arbitration is not going to be accepted, or that if it should be offered, there is no other outcome to be expected, than delay harmful to the one offering, the one foreseeing such results has a right of war against the other nation even though the conference or arbitration is not attempted" [1].

It can be seen from these last few lines that Wolff really permits war as a right under most circumstances. He says that "the right of war belongs to nations" [2]. On the question of the distinction between peoples with respect to war he holds that there is none. As he writes, "punitive war is legal for no nation against another because it professes atheism, or deism, or is idolatrous" [3].

The matter of the declaration of war was of concern to Wolff. He defines the declaration "as a public announcement of war made against a nation or its ruler by another nation or its ruler" [4]. There are two kinds of declarations of war, conditional and absolute. In an offensive war a declaration is required [5]. If the nation against whom the offensive war is being made, refuses to admit envoys, then the declaration is not required [6]. A defensive war does not require a declaration [7].

---

[1] *Ibid.*, p. 293.   [2] *Ibid.*, p. 313.   [3] *Ibid.*, p. 327.
[4] *Ibid.*, p. 364.   [5] *Ibid.*, p. 366.   [6] *Ibid.*, p. 369.
[7] *Ibid.*, p. 368.

It is now in point to give Wolff's distinction between a defensive and an offensive war.

> A defensive war is defined as one in which any one defends himself against another who brings war against him. But that is called an offensive war which is brought against another who was not thinking of bringing a war, or when any one assails another with arms [1].

Wolff considered the question of the just cause of war. "A just cause of war between nations arises only when a wrong has been done or is likely to be done" [2]. An unjust cause of war is, of course, the negative of this [3]. A just war is, then, a war with a just cause, and vice-versa, an unjust war an unjust cause [4]. He sums up his ideas on the just war by the following:

> Since there are only three just causes of war, namely (1) reparable wrong, (2) irreparable wrong, and (3) threatened wrong, which have the threefold purpose which is aimed at in a legal war, namely (1) the attainment of one's own or that which ought to be one's own, (2) the establishment of security, (3) the preventing of threatening danger or the warding off of injury; undoubtedly there are three kinds of just war which are distinguished by their different purposes. Therefore, since that is a defensive war in which the third is aimed at, a punitive war is which the second, is aimed at, it remains for us to give a name to the war also in which the first purpose is aimed at, and this war it has seemed best to call vindicative, war in imitation of the vindication of one's property [5].

Wolff next enters into a discussion of the two kinds of reasons given to support a war, justifying reasons and persuasive reasons. The former reasons "belong to the law of nature and nations, the latter are matters of statecraft or politics" [6]. Continuing the discussion

---

[1] *Ibid.*, p. 314.   [2] *Ibid.*   [3] Cf. *ibid.*, p. 315.
[4] *Ibid.*   [5] *Ibid.*, p. 316.   [6] *Ibid.*

of offensive and defensive wars. Wolff says that "a defensive war is just in which one defends oneself against another who brings an unjust war; but a defensive war is unjust if the offensive war is just" [1].

On the question of whether a war can be just on both sides, Wolff states that "war cannot be just on each side" [2]. If the case is a doubtful one then the matter should be submitted to arbitration, and if one side refuses to submit the case for arbitration the right of war belongs to the other side. Wolff puts it more accurately in the following: "For if in a doubtful case one nation should be unwilling to accept a conference for an amicable agreement or compromise, or for submission to arbiters consequently also if it should refuse to accept fair conditions offered to it the right of war against the one unwilling to accept belongs to the other, that thus the former may be driven to a compromise by force of arms" [3]. Of course, it should be pointed out that this allows many loopholes. For instance, who is to determine whether the conditions offered the demanding nation are fair? Wolff specifically lists certain things which are unjust causes of war. Among them are pleasure [4], utility [5], fear of a neighboring nation [6], and preservation of the equilibrium of nations [7].

The subject of neutrality was also considered by Wolff. With natural law as the basis of his system, he founds neutrality upon the law of nature. In his words,

[1] *Ibid.*, p. 320.   [2] *Ibid.*, p. 324.   [3] *Ibid.*, p. 322.
[4] *Ibid.*, pp. 318–9.   [5] *Ibid.*, pp. 316–8, 331.
[6] *Ibid.*, pp. 328–9.   [7] *Ibid.*, p. 332.

he says: "It is allowable by nature for any nation to be neutral in war if it should be of interest of the state rather to abstain from war than to involve itself in it should the reason for the war be doubtful" [1].

This permission granted to a nation to abstain from war if its own interest will be furthered is very much akin to the idea of war for reason of state. Wolff, however, does also imply that there is some kind of an obligation which third states have in a war. In one place, he states the point very specifically: "To a nation carrying on a just war it is allowable to send auxiliaries and subsidies and to aid it in a war in any manner, nay more, by nature nation is bound to nation as to those things, if that is possible; but for an unjust war none of these things may be done" [2]. It seems evident that under Wolff's system a nation is obligated to aid a state waging a just war, and is prohibited from helping the other nation. Neutrality can only exist when it is to the interest of the state to remain neutral or when the justice of the war is doubtful.

Wolff discussed time limitations on war as illustrated by truces [3], and place limitations in the form of treaties of neutrality [4]. He adds nothing new, however, to the literature on this aspect of the subject.

One of the most enthusiastic students of Wolff's famous work, *Jus Gentium Methodo Scientifica Pertractatum*, was Emer de Vattel (1714–1767) [5]. He was

---

[1] *Ibid.*, p. 347.   [2] *Ibid.*, p. 337.
[3] Cf. *ibid.*, pp. 471–4, 476–7.   [4] Cf. *ibid.*, pp. 346–9.
[5] Cf. Gidel, "Droit et Devoirs des Nations", *op. cit.*, pp. 577–85; Albert de Lapradelle, "Introduction" in E. de Vattel, *Le Droit des Gens* (Washington: Carnegie Institution, 1916), III, iii–iv.

so impressed by this work that he translated and adapted that portion which dealt with international relations [1]. It is in the very work of popularizing in a readable form this complex and pedantic book of Wolff that Vattel made his most significant contribution to international law. The result was his *Le Droit des Gens* (1758) [2]. The fact that Vattel was a cultivated and accomplished diplomat in the service of the King of Saxony contributed substantially to the success of his adaptive work. It states the law of nations with a comprehension which had no equal since Grotius [3]. It gains additional significance in that it combines the schools of reason and custom into a collective presentation of international law.

Vattel does not take over in its entirety the system of Wolff. The latter visualized a kind of world state (*Civitas Maxima*) to which all the nations belonged. What Vattel called the voluntary law of nations, Wolff saw as flowing from the world state. Vattel differs from his teacher in the respect that he denies the existence of a voluntary law of nations emanating from anything like a world state. He defines international law as follows: "The Law of Nations is the science of the rights which exist between Nations or States, and of the obligations corresponding to these rights" [4]. There are two main branches of the law of nations; the necessary or natural law of nations, and

---

[1] *Ibid.*, p. vii.

[2] *The Law of Nations*, English translation by Charles G. Fenwick (Washington: Carnegie Institution, 1916), Vol. III.

[3] Cf. Westlake, *op. cit.*, pp. 76–7.

[4] Vattel, *Law of Nations*, III, 3.

the positive law of nations. The former category comprises "those precepts which the natural law dictates to States" [1]. The positive law of nations proceeds from the agreement of nations. It is divided into three parts: "the voluntary law from their presumed consent, the conventional law from their express consent, and the customary law from their tacit consent" [2]. Vattel implies that the necessary law can be modified by the voluntary law [3]. "War is that state in which we prosecute our rights by force" [4]. By this definition he regards war both as a condition and as an instrument. He wrote further: "Public war is that which takes place between Nations or sovereigns, which is carried on in the name of the public authority and by its order. It is public war of which we treat here" [5].

The right to make war belongs exclusively to the sovereign. Concerning this Vattel wrote: "The right to decide whether a nation has a just subject of complaint, whether the circumstances are such as to justify the use of armed force, whether prudence will allow such action to be taken or whether the welfare of the state requires it this right, I say, is one of so important a nature that it can belong only to the body of the nation, or to the sovereign who represents it" [6]. A declaration of war Vattel holds is necessary in order to prevent as a last resort the use of arms. It is, as it were, a final threat [7]. He said that this is the regular

---

[1] *Ibid.*, p. 4.   [2] *Ibid.*, p. 9.   [3] *Ibid.*
[4] *Ibid.*, p. 235.   [5] *Ibid.*   [6] *Ibid.*   [7] *Ibid.*, p. 254.

practice of European states [1]. Vattel follows the Grotian classification of the declaration of war into two groups. The first is the simpler declaration, which exists "when justice has been demanded in vain" [2]. The second is the conditional declaration which is characterized by the demand for satisfaction (as the Romans called it, the *rerum repetitio*) accompanied by the announcement that unless this be made, war will be declared [3]. On the manner of making the declaration, Vattel wrote: "The declaration of war must be published to the State to which it is made. This is all that the natural law of Nations requires" [4]. If a nation has established the custom of declaring war by certain other formalities, it is obliged to do so unless it makes known its intention to the contrary [5]. The declaration can be made any time up to the beginning of hostilities. In certain cases, the declaration of war can be dispensed with. A defensive war does not necessitate a declaration, but most sovereigns hardly ever fail to declare war [6]. Even in an offensive war, a declaration is sometimes not required. This is in the case where the offending state refuses to admit the heralds of the offended nation to declare the war.

Vattel defines defensive war as follows: "A State which takes up arms to repel the attack of an enemy carries on a defensive war" [7]. The purpose of a defensive war is self-defense. With more complexity, an offensive war is defined. "A State which is the first to take up arms, and which attacks a nation living at

---

[1] *Ibid.*   [2] *Ibid.*   [3] *Ibid.*   [4] *Ibid.*, p. 255.
[5] *Ibid.*   [6] *Ibid.*   [7] *Ibid.*, p. 236.

peace with it, carries on an offensive war" [1]. Its purpose is not one but several. The purpose of an offensive war differs from the various interests of nations, but on the whole, it concerns either the enforcement of certain rights or their protection [2]. They are: (1) to obtain something to which a state lays claim, (2) to punish a nation for an injury received, (3) to forestall an injury which is about to be inflicted upon it, and (4) to avert a danger which seems to be threatening [3].

The just cause of war is an extension of three notions. "We may say, therefore, in general, that the foundation or the cause of every just war is an injury either already received, or threatening" [4]. An unjust war is, consequently, the opposite of this, namely when a nation has not received an injury or is not threatened [5]. The "lawful object of every war" is to avenge or to prevent an injury [6]. Vattel sums it up as follows: "Hence we can lay down clearly this threefold object of lawful war: (1) to obtain what belongs to us or what is due to us; (2) to provide for our future security by punishing the aggressor or the offender; (3) to defend ourselves, or to protect ourselves from injury by repelling unjust attacks" [7].

It is necessary in a just war to have the just cause supported by the proper motives. These are expediency, advisability, and prudence [8]. A war might have a just cause and still not be a just war. This would be so in the case where the war has an evil motive. If it does

[1] Ibid.   [2] Ibid.   [3] Ibid.   [4] Ibid., p. 243.
[5] Ibid., p. 244.   [6] Ibid.   [7] Ibid.   [8] Ibid.

not relate to the welfare of the state, it is an evil motive. With the concept of the welfare of the state, we find Vattel continuing the sixteenth century idea of the reason of state.

Vattel discusses another aspect of this central problem of the just war. It is in reference to the nature of justice and injustice of defensive and offensive war. A defensive war is just when it is carried on not only against an "unjust aggressor", but also against an aggressor which originally had a just cause [1]. This is in a situation where the defending state offered due satisfaction to the aggressor who refused to accept it.

An offensive war is just, both "in a manifestly good cause" and "in a doubtful cause". In the former instance it is just, when it exists to enforce some right, which cannot be done except by the "use of arms" [2]. "Necessity is the sole warrant for the use of force" [3]. In the second instance, it is just, if one party to the dispute asks that the question be submitted to discussion, and if it is not settled by that means, or by a fair compromise, and if the other party refuses to avail itself of this method then the other side is justified in beginning a defensive war [4].

Vattel discusses the question of an injury threatening a state. One form of a threatening injury is the aggrandizement of a neighboring power [5]. This alone is not sufficient to count as a threatening injury. It is, however, in the case where it is accompanied by "evidence of injustice, general pride, ambition, or a

---

[1] *Ibid.*, p. 246.   [2] *Ibid.*   [3] *Ibid.*
[4] *Ibid.*, pp. 246–7.   [5] *Ibid.*, p. 248.

desire to dominate over its neighbors"[1]. Another form of threat is the uniting of two strong states or of a sovereign maltreating other states, on the theory that if he maltreats others, he will maltreat you. Still another form is the preparation of a neighboring sovereign for war[2]. All of these cases which constitute a just cause for war, may be resolved to one fact, which is, that anything that attempts to break up the balance of power is a just cause for war.

Vattel takes up the traditional problem of whether a war can be just on both sides. He holds that in general, it can be just only on one side[3]. This is provided that the justice of the cause is obvious. When the cause is doubtful, and the contending parties are each acting in good faith, a war can be legitimate "on both sides provided that the cause has not been decided"[4]. Vattel used the doctrine of invincible ignorance in his reasoning[5].

It is worth pointing out here that Vattel made an interesting compromise on the question of whether a war could be just on both sides. What he held, as given in the above paragraph, he did according to the necessary or natural law of nations. This is modified to some extent by the voluntary law of nations. According to the law, "regular war, as regards its effects must be accounted just on both sides"[6]. Here is found a distinction which runs through the literature of the

---

[1] *Ibid.*, p. 249.   [2] *Ibid.*, pp. 249 ff.
[3] *Ibid.*, p. 251.   [4] *Ibid.*, p. 247.
[5] *Ibid.*: "But if his conduct is the result of invincible ignorance or error, the injustice of the war is not imputed to him".
[6] *Ibid.*, p. 305.

just war. A legal war in the sense of the voluntary law of nations is one that is determined by "the presence of the elements constituting a regular war" [1]. Vattel specifically states that the legality of a war according to the voluntary law of nations does not depend upon the justice of the cause [2]. The voluntary law of nations does not, however, excuse an aggressor with an unjust cause of war from his violation of the law of nature even though his conduct is legal [3].

What Vattel wrote concerning neutrality is somewhat confused. "Neutral nations are those which take no part in a war, and remain friends of both parties, without favoring either side to the prejudice of the other" [4]. A neutral nation may grant the passage of belligerent troops through its territory, provided that the object of the passage is a just one, or in other words that the war be a just one [5]. If the neutral had to decide between the welfare of the state and aiding the just belligerent in the matter of the passage of troops, Vattel holds that the neutral "is not called upon to draw down evil on his own head in order to protect that of another" [6]. On the other hand, the neutral state may refuse passage to a nation which intends to carry on an unjust war [7]. In the chapter preceding the one on neutrality, Vattel states firmly that: "It is lawful and praiseworthy to assist in every way a Nation which is carrying on a just war; and such assistance even becomes a duty for every nation which can give it without injury to itself. But no assistance may be given

---

[1] *Ibid.*   [2] Cf. *ibid.*, p. 305.   [3] *Ibid.*
[4] *Ibid.*, p. 268.   [5] *Ibid.*, p. 278.   [6] *Ibid.*   [7] *Ibid.*

to one who wages an unjust war" [1]. He obviously believes that the third state is required to go to war against a nation which has an unjust cause and to support the one which has a just cause [2]. We have seen that he considered it wrong to concede an unjust belligerent passage, and we shall see that he also held that such a belligerent should not be furnished with aid by a treaty of alliance. Vattel wrote: "If the war which a prince is waging, or is about to wage, is unjust, we are not allowed to enter into an alliance with him, since we may not give our aid to an unjust cause" [3].

Vattel discusses a limitation on war with respect to time, that is, the truce. "A truce or suspension of hostilities does not terminate the war; it merely suspends its operations" [4]. He says that a truce is either partial or general. "By the former hostilities cease merely in certain places, as between a town and an army besieging it; by the latter hostilities cease throughout the whole area of the war" [5].

Summary. — The great number of wars in the eighteenth century created certain practical problems. Some of these resulted in more clear thinking on the question of the legal position of war; others made little impression on the contemporary writers on international law. Although wars were being fought in the Orient and in the New World, between civilized states, on one side, and primitive communities on the other,

---

[1] *Ibid.*, p. 262.

[2] *Ibid.*: "It is always commendable to assist a just cause when we can do so; but to aid an unjust Nation is to participate in its crime and to become ourselves guilty of injustice".

[3] *Ibid.*   [4] *Ibid.*, p. 322.   [5] *Ibid.*

the notion of the distinction between peoples with respect to war was not present in some of the works of the publicists. Bynkershoek tells us that a war may be lawful without a formal declaration. His attitude is shared by de Martens. On the other hand Moser says that international law requires a declaration of war. Wolff lays down the rule that in an offensive war a declaration is required, while in a defensive war it is not. Vattel states that a declaration is necessary. He even goes so far as to say that this is the regular practice of European states. Of the many different points of view, it is interesting to note that a positive writer, Bynkershoek, who based international law on custom, states that international law does not require a declaration of war. And such was the practice of the century.

The notion of the just war and the just cause of war, although not apparent in the practice of the century, was most evident in the writings of the publicists, Bynkershoek excepted. This international lawyer had too much of a practical turn of mind to include in his work a statement of the doctrine of the just cause of war. In other positive writers we find references to this idea. Moser refers to "war reasons" — necessity and custom. Almost any war, however, can be justified under these conditions. De Martens like Moser does not specifically discuss the doctrine of the just cause of war as such. He merely established the principle that war is justified only when there is an actual or threatened violation of a right. It is worthwhile to mention here that de Martens held as some of the

Renaissance humanists and reformers did that states can make war only when they have attempted to settle the dispute by amicable means.

A just cause, Wolff defines, as a wrong done or likely to be done. This is essentially the same concept as the one of de Martens. Wolff differs from both Bynkershoek and de Martens who wrote that war is just on both sides by saying that war cannot be just on either side. Wolff makes a remarkable contribution by holding that if a nation refuses to submit the dispute to conference, or arbitration, then the other side has the legal right of war. Vattel, Wolf's famous disciple, gives the same definition of the just cause of war, an injury received or threatened. And like his mentor, he holds that a war can be just only on one side.

Perhaps the most interesting development of the practice and theory of the legality of war in the eighteenth century is found in that aspect which refers to neutrality and its closely associated problem, the duty of third states to go to war. The position of absolute neutrality was best stated by a national of a country desiring the acceptance of the neutral status — Bynkershoek, a Dutchman, who worked out a very clear notion of neutrality. He definitely states that it is not the function of a third party to sit in judgment on a dispute between nations with the purpose of joining one side or the other. Both Moser and de Martens agree with Bynkershoek in this position.

In contrast to this attitude is the point of view of Wolff. This writer coming from Prussia, a strong power, naturally would not be so unequivocal in his stand on neutrality. In fact, Wolff goes so far in his attitude as to require states to take sides with the nation carrying on a just war. Wolff, however, said that states are required to do this except when it is not against their interest. This reservation still leaves the question undecided. Vattel seems to contradict himself even more than Wolff does on this question. At one point he says that a neutral is not bound to give aid to the state with the just cause and at another point he says that it is a duty. Wolff and Vattel both mention truces as a means of limiting war, but they do not set up any general system of time restrictions before the beginning of hostilities.

CHAPTER VI

CONCLUSION

The legal position of war varied greatly from the time of Plato to that of Vattel. War was considered the normal situation in the international relations of ancient Greece, yet a state of war was beginning to be regarded as a special legal situation. The requirement of a formal declaration of war was recognized and often practiced. There were limitations on war with respect to time. Among these were the prohibition of warfare during Greek religious festivals and athletic contests, and the regulation of war by treaties of peace for a specific number of years. War was also forbidden to be waged around certain temples and sanctuaries. To be sure, what international law there was in the time of Plato, appears to have been founded chiefly upon religious customs and practices. The observance by the Greeks of these customs and practices with reference to war is evidence, however, that the Greeks had some notions of what was and was not permitted in commencing a war (*jus ad bellum*). Certain thinkers, especially Aristotle, began to distinguish just from unjust causes of war. A distinction between peoples with respect to war was apparent, as the Hellenes considered the laws of war (*jus in bello*) applicable only to wars among themselves and not to wars fought with

6

outside states whose peoples were classed as barbarians. Hostilities could be commenced with the barbarian states at any time, and could be conducted without mercy. It might be interjected that during the two thousand years that have elapsed from the age of Pericles to the age of Mussolini, this aspect of the legal position of war has changed very little.

Like the Greeks who made the distinction of Hellenes and non-Hellenes with respect to war, the Romans distinguished between themselves and foreigners, or *hostes*. The word, *hostis*, meant enemy as well as foreigner. The Roman attitude toward the legal position of war is indicated by their formulation and administration of the *jus fetiale*. This contained, among other things, an elaborate set of rules concerning the declaration of war. Some students of the *jus fetiale* believe that the fetial college considered whether there was a just cause of war. It is certain that the fetial college advised as to the formalities for initiating war. This institution greatly influenced Roman thought on war.

In the works of Cicero, we find very precise definitions of just and unjust war. It is the present writer's conclusion that the contribution of Cicero on this question cannot be too greatly emphasized. Many students of the just war theory are inclined to commence their discussions with the ideas of the mediaeval churchmen, assuming that the concept of the just war was an ecclesiastical invention. It seems evident, however, that this concept was worked out in antiquity, and probably was first formulated by Cicero.

His definition of a just war seems to imply the notion of a just cause of war, for instance among his works are the following statements: ".... those wars are unjust which are undertaken without cause, and only those wars waged for revenge or defense can be just", and ".... no war is undertaken in the ideal state except in defense of its honor or its safety".

In antiquity, the sphere of the state was unlimited; the state was virtually omnipotent in all matters. In the middle ages, the sphere of the state was limited by the power of the church. The state appeared to be subservient to the church. In the light of this condition, it is obvious that the church played an important role in the legal control of war. In the last days of the Roman Empire when the church was founded, the conflict of interest between the church and state became apparent in the question of making war. The state was continuing the traditional doctrine of the immutable right of waging war; while the church imbued with Christian ethics was beginning to challenge the ancient doctrine of making war. Both church and state were commencing to follow natural law and divine law in the ascertainment of political and legal decisions. The questions then were, "what did the law of nature say about waging war", and "what did the law of God say about waging war". In the later Roman Empire, an outstanding problem confronting the church was, "is it lawful for Christians to fight for the Empire". This question brings out the conflicts of loyalties at this period of history. Biblical injunctions forbade Christians to take up arms as soldiers. At first,

Christians refused to fight, but when the Empire was threatened by invasion of the barbarians from the north, the problem had to be solved.

From this historical background came the patristic writers. Greatest of them was Saint Augustine who is generally accredited by most students to be the originator of the mediaeval theory of the just war. A few scholars believe that Saint Ambrose rather than Saint Augustine invented the just war theory. If the paternity of this brain child must be established, Cicero has as much claim to it as any other thinker. The patristic writers and the mediaeval schoolmen approached the question, "is it lawful for Christians to fight", by studying the facts respecting a particular war, the *casus belli*. In doing this, they would make a very careful analysis of the moral (natural law) aspects of a proposed war. A defensive war was usually considered justifiable. It was the offensive war which became the main subject for discussion. For a period of a thousand years, the leading thinkers on the subject, Saint Augustine, Isidore of Seville, and Saint Thomas Aquinas placed particular stress on the question of the just war. According to their theory which characterized the Middle Ages, war was only justifiable if it were used as an instrument of justice. In other words war might be a means of righting a wrong. The just war, then, was a war used to promote justice. It is evident that the mediaeval writers had a conception of international justice defined by natural and divine law, and maintained if necessary by military force. The just war was one which had (1) a proper motive, (2) a just cause, (3) the element of proportionality, i.e., the good that it would accomplish would at least offset the damage that it would do, and (4) a declaration by the proper authority.

It was this last condition that was of particuliar concern to the mediaeval legists. They took for granted the writings of the earlier churchmen, who concerned themselves with the underlying moral question of whether or not a particular war had a just cause. What was of paramount importance to the legists was the problem of under whose authority was the war instituted. This problem faced the political-legal thinking of the time. The immediate task was the unification of Christendom. The legal rationalization of this problem on the basis of the political-ecclesiastical organization of the later Middle Ages resulted in the doctrine that a war could be declared only by a legitimate authority. Legitimate authority came to mean only the Pope or the Emperor. Lignano even more than Hostiensis was interested in considering a war just or unjust from the standpoint of the political organization of the time. He developed a very ingenious argument to prove the temporal supremacy of the papacy. This was, of course, another way of saying that a just war could be authorized only by the Pope. Other thinkers of this period did not go as far in supporting the omnipotence of the Pope, as did Lignano. Dante, for instance, in his *De Monarchia* held that the Holy Roman Emperor was the legal ruler of the world, and alone competent to authorize military force.

The legists were anxious to prove that the Crusades were just wars. They resorted to the concept of the distinction between peoples with respect to war to prove their point. They held that there were only two kinds of people in the world, Christians and infidels. On the one hand, the legists wanted to put a stop to feudal warfare which they considered unjust because it was sanctioned neither by the Pope nor by the Emperor, and on the other hand, they wanted to justify the Crusades.

Just before the Crusades, there developed such institutions as the Truce and Peace of God which limited war with respect to time and place. During the Crusades, the French *Quarantaine du Roi* and the German *Landfriede* operated in a way similar to the Truce of God. These institutions were designed to reduce the amount of incessant feudal warfare which characterized the international relations of the Middle Ages. It is worth recalling that these institutions had their prototypes in the Hellenic period.

In the fifteenth century and onward, the doctrine of legitimate authority coincided with the emergence of the patrimonial state and the idea of absolute sovereignty. Finally, it evolved into the stage where the right to make war was considered one of the chief ends of the state. By the fifteenth century the Emperor was considered sovereign over his own Empire, but not over the world. There were other sovereign states on the political horizon. These new states also had the legitimate authority to make war. The power of the papacy had waned, and by the fifteenth century, the

Pope had only religious power. No longer was he, as Lignano once tried to make him, the temporal as well as the spiritual ruler of the world.

The just war theory had now moved to a new setting. In the fifteenth and sixteenth centuries, there appeared the notion that a war could be just on both sides. This was reasoned out best in the doctrine of *probablism*. While this doctrine still retained the old notion that objectively speaking, a war could be just on only one side, it held the new idea that subjectively speaking, a war could be just on both sides, provided that there was *invincible ignorance* as to a side having or not having a just cause of war. The doctrine of *probablism* spelled the death of the just war theory. It is true, however, that the early *classical* writers on international law, who first treated international law as a subject separate from anything else, spent much time in their works discussing the theory of the just war. It is also true that the Spanish school of international law headed by Victoria, based their discussion upon the scholastic doctrines in considering the legal position of war.

Victoria has been called the last of the mediaevalists and the first of the moderns. He believed in the just war theory. He delivered a polemic showing that there was no distinction between the Spanish and the Indians of the New World, in respect to war. This was definitely opposed to the practice of his government. His moralist approach with its emphasis on international justice is the mediaeval strain which appears in his work. He is first of the moderns because he saw the development of a specialized subject matter of law as practized between nations. The evidence for this new law was positive. Positivism in international law has meant the reliance upon treaties and international custom as the main source for international law. While Victoria is not exactly considered a positivist in international law, he is certainly more than a moralist. He was the first real student of international law, per se.

With the passing of Victoria, the notion that there was a well defined rule of international justice was abandoned. The idea that a war could be just on both sides took the place of the mediaeval theory that only one side possessed a just cause. With this new doctrine, the sovereign could act both as an accuser and as a judge. This development was made inevitable by the rise of the modern state system. An outstanding political thinker who rationalized this new system was Machiavelli. A strong supporter of the nationalistic state, he identified the theory of war for reason of state with the theory of the just war. The reason of state was necessity; a just war, then, was a war that was necessary. Another exponent of the idea of the national state was Bodin. He held the same doctrine of a just war as did Machiavelli, but reached it by a different method. The former used *Realpolitik*, while the latter relied on his political theory of absolute sovereignty. The mediaeval theory of the just war had in it the notion of necessity. A war had to be necessary to be just. The definition of reason of state as necessity, as expressed for instance by Machiavelli, meant something more than necessity. It meant utility. A war in the terms of Machiavelli was just, if it were useful to the state.

In contradistinction, the mediaeval theory of necessity of war was that it could be resorted to only if there were no other methods to settle the dispute. With our Hague Court of Arbitration, our Permanent Court of International Justice, and our League of Nations, we have difficulty in visualizing the absence of pacific methods for the settlement of international disputes. There seems to have been a much smaller number of methods in the mediaeval period than in the modern one. The mediaeval doctrine of necessity should be viewed in this perspective.

The significance of Grotius in the history of political theory is that he combined the *jus gentium* with the *jus naturale*. As for his significance in the history of the legal position of war, it can be said that he more than any writer up to his time gave war a juridical status in international law. Unlike Suarez, who believed that war was a historical fact and sooner or later would disappear, Grotius held that war would probably always be present because it was a right under international law. Although Grotius was shocked by the ravages and horrors of the Thirty Years' War, he did not outlaw war from his system of law. He did not disagree with the mediaeval moralists who regarded war as an instrument of justice, but he did not hold with them in their doctrine of the existence of an objective standard of justice. The Grotian method of controlling war was to make war subservient to international law. He reoriented the just war theory into an entirely new setting. A just war was one made in defense of the law of nations. Grotius perceived the development of international law, and regarded war as an instrument to maintain this new law. In this respect, he was not wholly unlike the mediaeval churchmen who viewed war as an instrument to promote international morality or justice.

International law writing after Grotius has dealt more with *jus in bello* than *jus ad bellum*. Discussion of the rules of warfare and the laws of neutrality occupy a much larger part of the texts in international law than do expositions of the circumstances which are supposed to justify a war. There was, nevertheless, in the works on international law since Grotius some mention of the problem of the legal position of war. In the seventeenth and eighteenth centuries, there were two schools of thought in treating this problem. One school is represented by the positivists, chiefly Zouche, Bynkershoek, Moser, and de Martens. To the other school belong the naturalists, principally Pufendorf, Wolff, and Vattel.

International law in the nineteenth and the first two decades of the twentieth centuries has followed the positivists. They hold that custom is the basis of international law. The concept of the just war does not exist in their interpretation of international law. Such a concept belongs in the realm of international ethics. It is the practice of states that makes law and, since the history of the modern world has been filled with wars fought under all sorts of circumstances, the positivists hold that it is useless to discuss justifications which do not exist in practice. They even go so far as to maintain that, since international practice does not show that declarations of war are always given before the commencement of hostilities, international law does not require them to be given. On the other hand, the naturalists in international law, especially Wolff, have redefined the notion of the just war. Their definition approximates the notion of a "just" war contained in the Geneva Protocol. An understanding of a just war is possible by defining an unjust war. An unjust war is one commenced by a state without having first submitted its dispute to some method of pacific settlement. Wolff even laid down a very ingenious theory of the responsibility of states for the preservation of the criterion of the just war.

It can be said in summary that the *jus ad bellum* has varied with the political conditions of various historical epochs. The Hellenic period witnessed its emergence from a set of religious customs and a philosophy of political ethics. In Rome the legal practices sharpened distinctions and gave war for the first time a definite legal position. The Middle Ages developed the doctrine that war was an instrument of justice. It was legal if its end was morally right. The Renaissance and Reformation saw the *jus ad bellum* change into an expression of modern nationalism. The legal position of war was adjusted to the utilitarian position of war. This was partly changed by the international law writing of the seventeenth and eighteenth centuries which had as its purpose the control of war through its conformity to a new kind of law, international law. In the nineteenth and early twentieth centuries little interest was displayed in the control of war by allotting to war a legal position. It is only very recently that the question of regulating war by juridical means has again been seriously approached in the interpretation of the Covenant of the League of Nations and the Kellogg-Briand Pact.

———

BIBLIOGRAPHY

SOURCES

AMBROSE. "De Officiis", *Patrologiae Cursus Completus*, Vol. XVI·
Parisiis: Apud Garnier Fratres, Editores et J. P. Migne,
Successores, 1886. Pp. 26–198.

ARISTOTLE. "Politics", *Works of Aristotle*, Vol. X. Edited by W. D.
Ross. Oxford: Clarendon Press, 1921. Pp. 1252*a*–1342*b*.

———. "Rhetoric", *Works of Aristotle*, Vol. XI. Edited by W. D.
Ross. Oxford: Clarendon Press, 1921. Pp. 1354*a*–1419*b*.

AUGUSTINE. "Contra Faustum", *Patrologiae Cursus Completus*, Vol.
XLII. Parisiis: Apud Garnier Fratres, Editores et J. P. Migne,
Successores, 1886. Pp. 209–518.

———. "Quaestionum in Heptateuchen", *Patrologiae Cursus Completus*, Vol. XXXIV. Parisiis: Apud Garnier Fratres, Editores
et J. P. Migne, Successores, 1886. Pp. 547–823.

AYALA, B. *De Jure et Officilis Bellicis et Disciplina Militari Libri*.
Translated by John Pawley Bate. Vol. II. Washington, D. C.:
Carnegie Institution, 1912.

BACON, FRANCIS. *Essays*. Edited by Mary A. Scott. New York:
Charles Scribner's Sons, 1908.

———. *Works*. Edited by James Spedding. London: Longman, 1874.

BYNKERSHOEK, C. *De Dominio Maris Dissertatio*. Translated by
Ralph Van Deman Magoffin. New York: Oxford University
Press, 1923.

———. *Quaestionum Juris Publici Libri Duo*. Translated by Tenney
Frank. Vol. II. Oxford: Clarendon Press, 1930.

CICERO. *De Officiis*. Translated by Walter Miller. New York: The
Macmillan Co., 1921.

———. *De Republica*. Translated by G. H. Sabine and S. B. Smith.
Columbus, Ohio: The Ohio State University Press, 1929.

Les Conventions de Declarations de la Haye de 1899 et 1907. New York:
Oxford University Press, 1918.

Corpus Juris Civilis. Edited by Christoph. Henr. Freiesieben, Coloniae Munatiane, Suptibus E. and J. R. Thunrisiorum Fratum
MDCCXXXV.

DANTE. *De Monarchia.* Edited and translated by Aurelia Henry. Boston: Houghton, Mifflin & Co., 1904.

Decretum Gratiani, Corpus Juris Canonici. Editio Lipsiensis, Secunda post A. E. Richteri, etc. Leipzig: Tauchnitz, 1879.

ERASMUS, DESIDERIUS. *Enchiridion Militis Christiani.* Roterodamo: Lugduni Batavorum ex Officina Johannis Maire, 1504(?).

——. *The Complaint of Peace.* Translated by T. Paynell. Chicago: The Open Court Publishing Co., 1917.

GENTILI, ALBERICO. *De Jure Belli Libri Tres.* Translated by J. C. Rolfe, Vol. II. Oxford: Clarendon Press, 1933.

——. *Hispanicae Advocationis Libri Duo.* Translated by F. F. Abbott. New York: Oxford Press, 1921.

GROTIUS, HUGO. *De Jure Belli ac Pacis.* Translated by Francis W. Kelsey. Vol. II. Oxford: Clarendon Press, 1925.

ISIDORE OF SEVILLE. *Etymologiarum sive Originum.* Edited by W. M. Lindsay. Oxford: Clarendon Press, 1911.

IVO OF CHARTRES. "Decreti", *Patrologiae Cursus Completus,* Vol. CLXI. Parisiis: Apud Garnier Fratres, Editores et J. P. Migne, Successores, 1886. Pp. 7–27.

JOWETT, B. (trans.). *Thucydides.* Vol. II. Oxford: Clarendon Press, 1900.

LIGNANO, JOHANNIS DE. *De Bello, De Represalis, et De Duello.* Edited by T. E. Holland, and trans. by J. L. Brierly. Oxford: Carnegie Institution, 1917.

LUTHER, MARTIN. "Ob Kriegsleute auch in seligem lande sein können", *Works of Martin Luther,* Vol. V. Translated by C. M. Jacobs. Philadelphia: A. J. Holman Company, 1931. Pp. 32–74.

MACHIAVELLI, NICCOLO. "Art of War". *Machiavelli,* Vol. I. *Tudor Translations,* Vol. XXXIX. Translated by Peter Whitehorne. London: D. Nutt ,1905. Pp. 27–232.

——. *Prince.* Translated by N. H. Thomson. 3d ed. Oxford: Clarendon Press, 1913.

——. "Thoughts of a Statesman", *The Historical, Political and Diplomatic Writings of Niccolo Machiavelli,* Vol. II. Boston: J. R. Osgood and Company, 1882. Pp. 433–464.

DE MARTENS, GEORGE FRIEDRICH. *Précis du Droit des Gens Moderne de l'Europe.* Translated by William Cobbett. Philadelphia: Thomas Bradford, 1795.

MORE, THOMAS. "Utopia" in Henry Morley, *Ideal Commonwealths.* London: Colonial Press, 1901. Pp. 3–99.

MOSER, JOHANN JACOB. *Versuch des neuesten Europäischen Völkerrechts.* Vol. IX. Frankfort am Main: Varrentropp Sohn und Wenner, 1779.

PLATO. "Laws", *Dialogues*, Vol. V. Translated by B. Jowett. 3d ed. Oxford: Oxford University Press, 1892. Pp. 1–361.

——. "Protagoras", *Dialogues*, Vol. I. Translated by B. Jowett. 3d ed. Oxford: Oxford University Press, 1892. Pp. 129–187.

——. "Republic", *Dialogues*, Vol. III. Translated by B. Jowett. 3d ed. Oxford: Oxford University Press, 1892. Pp. 1–338.

PUFENDORF, SAMUEL VON. *De Jure Naturae et Gentium*. Translated by Basil Kennett. London: J. Walthoe et al., 1729.

——. *Elementorum Jurisprudentiae Universalis Libri Duo*. Translated by W. A. Oldfather. Vol. II. Oxford: Clarendon Press, 1931.

——. *De Officio Hominis et Avis Juxta Legem Naturalem Libri Duo*. Translated by F. G. Moore. Vol. II. New York: Oxford University Press, 1927.

RACHEL, SAMUEL. *De Jure Naturae et Gentium Dissertationes*. Translated by J. P. Bate. Vol. II. Washington, D. C.: Carnegie Institution, 1916.

THATCHER, O. J., and McNEAL, F. H. *Source Book for Mediaeval History*. New York: C. Scribner's Sons, 1905.

THOMAS AQUINAS. *Summa Theologica*. Translated by Fathers of the English Dominican Province. New York: Benziger Brothers, 1917.

TEXTOR, JOHANN WOLFGANG. *Synopsis Juris Gentium*. Translated by John Pawley Bate. Vol. II. Washington: Carnegie Institution, 1916.

VATTEL, EMER DE. *The Law of Nations*. Translated by Charles G. Fenwick. Vol. III. Washington: Carnegie Institution, 1916.

VICTORIA, FRANCISCUS DE. *De Indis et De Jure Belli Relectiones*. Translated by H. F. WRIGHT. Washington: Carnegie Institution, 1917.

WOLFF, CHRISTIAN. *Jus Gentium Methodo Scientifica Pertractatum*. Translated by J. H. Drake. Vol. II. Oxford: Clarendon Press, 1934.

ZOUCHE, RICHARD. *Juris et Judicii Feciales sine Juris inter Gentes, et Quaestionum de Eodem Explicatio*. Translated by J. L. Brierly. Vol. II. Washington: Carnegie Institution, 1911.

BOOKS

ALLEN, J. W. *A History of the Political Thought in the Sixteenth Century*. New York: The Dial Press, 1928.

BARKER, E. *Greek Political Theory*. 2d ed. London: Methuen & Co., 1925.

BEALES, A. C. F. *The History of Peace*. New York: Dial Press, 1931.
BREASTED, J. H. *Ancient Records of Egypt*. Vol. III. Chicago: University of Chicago Press, 1906.
BRUNNER, H. *Deutsche Rechtsgeschichte*. Vol. II. Leipzig: Von Duncker und Humboldt, 1892.
BURNELL, A. K. and HOPKINS, E. W. *The Ordinances of Manu*. Lecture VII. London: Kegan Paul, Trench, Tubner & Co., 1891.
BUSOLT, G. *Griechische Staatskunde*. Vol. II. München: Beck, 1926.
BUTLER, G., and MACCOBY, S. *The Development of International Law*. London: Longmans, Green & Co., 1926.
CADOUX, C. J. *The Early Christian Attitude toward War*. London: The Swarthmore Press, Ltd., 1919.
CALDWELL, W. E. *Hellenic Conceptions of Peace*. New York: Columbia University, 1919.
CAMPBELL, W. E. *More's Utopia and His Social Teaching*. London: Eyre and Spotteswoode, 1930.
Cambridge Mediaeval History. Vol. V. New York: Macmillan Co., 1926.
Cambridge Modern History. Vol. VI. New York: Macmillan Co., 1909.
CARLYLE, A. J. *A History of Mediaeval Political Theory in the West*. Vol. I. New York: G. P. Putnam's Sons, 1903.
CLARK, G. N. *The Seventeenth Century*. Oxford: Clarendon Press, 1929.
DICKINSON, E. D. *The Equality of States in International Law*. Cambridge: Harvard University Press, 1920.
DUNNING, W. A. *A History of Political Theories; Ancient and Medieval*. New York: Macmillan Co., 1923.
——. *A History of Political Theories, from Luther to Montesquieu*. New York: Macmillan & Co., 1927.
DYER, LOUIS. *Machiavelli and the Modern State*. Boston: Ginn & Co., 1904.
ENGELMAN, G. *Political Philosophy*. New York: Harpers, 1927.
FENWICK, C. G. *International Law*. 2d ed. New York: Century, 1934.
FERGUSON, W. S. *Greek Imperialism*. Boston: Houghton Mifflin Co., 1913.
FIGGE, ROBERT. *Georg Friedrich von Martens Sein Leben und seine Werke*. Inaugural-Dissertation. Gleiwiss: P. Hill's Buchdruckerei, 1914.
FRANK, T. *Roman Imperialism*. New York: Macmillan Co., 1914.
GETTELL, R. G. *History of Political Thought*. New York: Century, 1924.

GIERKE, O. *Political Theories of the Middle Ages.* Translated by F. W. Maitland. Cambridge: University Press, 1900.

GOEBEL, J. *The Equality of States.* New York: Columbia University Press, 1923.

GOMPERZ, T. *Greek Thinkers.* Vol. I. London: John Murray, 1906.

HALL, W. E. *Treatise on International Law.* 6th ed. Oxford: Clarendon Press, 1909.

HALLAM, H. *Introduction to the Literature of Europe.* New York: Harpers, 1841.

HASSALL, ARTHUR. *Balance of Power, 1715–1789.* London: Rivington's, 1922.

HEARNSHAW, F. J. C. *Social and Political Ideas of Some of the Great Thinkers of the Renaissance and the Reformation.* London: George C. Harrop & Co., 1925.

HELM, RUDOLPH, *Hugo Grotius.* Rostock: H. Warkenstiens, 1920.

HERSHEY, A. S. *Essentials of Public International Law.* 2d ed. New York: Macmillan Co., 1927.

HILL, D. J. *A History of Diplomacy in International Development of Europe.* Vol. I. New York: Longmans, Green & Co., 1905.

HOLDSWORTH, W. S. "The Common Law and Its Rivals", *History of the English Law.* Vol. V. Boston: Little, Brown & Co., 1924.

HOLLAND, T. E. *Lectures on International Law.* London: Sweet and Maxwell Ltd., 1933.

———. *Studies in International Law.* Oxford: Clarendon Press, 1898.

HUIZINGA, JOHAN. *Erasmus.* New York: C. Scribner's Sons, 1924.

JESSUP, PHILIP C., and DEAK, FRANCIS, *Neutrality, Its History Economics and Law.* Vol. I, *The Origins.* New York: Columbia University Press, 1935.

KAUTSKY KARL. *Thomas More and His Utopia.* London: H. & C. Black, 1927.

KELSEN, H. *Allgemeine Staatslehre.* Berlin: J. Springer, 1925.

KNIGHT, W. S. M. *Life and Works of Hugo Grotius.* London: Sweet and Maxwell, 1925.

LANGE, C. L. *Histoire de l'Internationalisme.* Kristiana: H. Aschenhoug & Co., 1919.

LAURENT, F. *Histoire du Droit des Gens et des Relations Internationales.* Vols. II and III. Gand: L. Hebbelynck, 1850–70.

LAWRENCE, T. J. *International Law.* 4th ed. Boston: D. C. Heath & Co., 1910.

LORIMER, JAMES. *The Institutes of the Law of Nations.* Edinburgh: William Blackwood and Sons, 1883.

LUCHAIRE, A. *Manuel des Institutions Françaises.* Paris: Hachette et Cie., 1892.

MARQUARDT, J. *Römische Staatsverwaltung*. Vol. III. Leipzig: S. Hirzel, 1885.

MASTERSON, P. V. *et al*. *Francisco Suarez, Addresses in Commemoration of his Contribution to International Law and Politics*. Washington, D. C.: H. F. Wright, 1933.

MEINECKE, F. *Die Idee der Staatsräson*. München und Berlin: Druck und Verlag von R. Oldenbourg, 1924.

——. *Weltbürgertum und Nationalstaat*. 5th ed. München und Berlin: Druck und Verlag von R. Oldenbourg, 1919.

MERRIAM, C. E. *History of the Theory of Sovereignty Since Rousseau*. New York: Columbia University, 1900.

MOWAT, R. B. *The Age of Reason*. Boston: Houghton, Mifflin Co., 1934.

——. *A History of European Diplomacy, 1451-1789*. London: Edwin Arnold & Co., 1928.

——. *European States System*. London: Oxford University Press, 1923.

MÜLLER–JOCHMUS, MAURITIUS, *Geschichte des Völkerrechts im Alterthum*. Leipzig: E. Keil & Co., 1848.

NEWMAN, W. L. *Politics of Aristotle*. Vol. I. Oxford: Clarendon Press, 1887.

NYS, E. *Le Droit de la Guerre et les Précurseurs de Grotius*. Bruxelles et Leipzig: C. Muquardt, 1882.

——. *Le Droit International*. Vol. III. Bruxelles: A. Castaigne, 1906.

——. *Les Origines du Droit International*. Paris: A. Castaigne, 1894.

OPPENHEIM, L. *International Law*. 4th ed. London: Longmans, Green and Co., 1928.

PHILLIPSON, C. *The International Law and Custom of Ancient Greece and Rome*. London: Macmillan & Co., 1911.

PLAPPERT, E. *Franz Suarez als Völkerrechtler*. Darmstadt: Edward Roether, 1914.

REGOUT, ROBERT, S. J. *La Doctrine de la Guerre Juste de Saint Augustin à Nos Jours*. Paris: A. Pedone, 1935.

ROMMEN, H. *Die Staatslehre des Franz Suarez S. J*. M. Gladbach, 1926.

ROSS, J. E. *Christian Ethics*. New York: The Devin-Adair Company, 1927.

RUSSELL, F. M. *Theories of International Relations*. New York: D. Appleton Century Co., 1936.

SCHUMAN, F. L. *International Politics*. New York: McGraw-Hill Book Company, 1933.

SCOTT, J. B. *The Catholic Conception of International Law.* Washington: Georgetown University Press, 1934.

——. *The Discovery of America and Its Influences on International Law.* Washington, D. C.: Catholic University, 1929.

——. *The Spanish Conception of International Law and of Sanctions.* Washington: Carnegie Endowment for International Peace, 1934.

——. *The Spanish Origins of International Law.* Washington, D. C.: Georgetown University, 1928.

——. *The Spanish Origin of International Law.* Part I, *Francisco de Vitoria and His Law of Nations.* Oxford: Clarendon Press, 1934.

SHOTWELL, J. T. *War as an Instrument of National Policy.* New York: Harcourt, Brace & Co., 1929.

SMITH, PRESERVED. *Age of the Reformation.* New York: Macmillan & Co., 1920.

——. *A History of Modern Culture.* New York: Macmillan, 1930.

——. *Erasmus.* New York: Harper and Brothers, 1923.

——. *Life and Letters of Martin Luther.* Boston: Houghton Mifflin, 1911.

STRATMAN, FRANZISKUS. *The Church and War.* New York: P. J. Kennedy and Sons, 1935.

STURZO, LUIGI. *The International Community and the Right of War.* New York: Richard R. Smith, Inc., 1930.

SYMONDS, J. A. *Renaissance in Italy.* New York: Henry Holt & Co., 1887.

TER MEULEN, JACOB. *Beitrag zur Geschichte der Internationalen Organisation 1300–1700.* Haag: Martinus Nijhoff, 1916.

THOMPSON, J. W. *Economic and Social History of the Middle Ages.* New York: Century Co., 1928.

TOURSCHER, F. E. *War and Peace in Saint Augustine's De Civitate Dei.* Washington: The Catholic Association for International Peace, 1934 (pamphlet).

TRELLES, C. BARCIA. *Francisco de Vitoria.* Madrid: Sección de Estudios Americanistas, 1928.

VANDERPOL, A. *La Doctrine Scolastique du Droit de la Guerre.* Paris: A Pedone, 1925.

VAN VOLLENHOVEN, CORNELIUS. *De Droit de Paix, de Iure Pacis.* La Haye: M. Nijhoff, 1932.

——. *On the Genesis of the De Jure Belli et Pacis* (Grotius, 1625). Amsterdam: Koninklijke Akademie, 1924.

——. *The Three Stages in the Evolution of the Law of Nations.* The Hague: Martinus Nijhoff, 1919.

VINOGRADOFF, Sir PAUL. *Outlines of Historical Jurisprudence.* Vol. II. Oxford: Oxford University Press, 1929.

VREELAND, H. *Hugo Grotius.* New York: Oxford University Press, 1917.

WALKER, T. A. *A History of the Law of Nations.* Vol. I. Cambridge: University Press, 1899.

WARING, L. H. *Political Theories of Martin Luther.* New York: G. P. Putnam's Sons, 1910.

WEHBERG, H. *The Outlawry of War.* Washington, D. C.: Carnegie Endowment for International Peace, 1931.

WESTLAKE, JOHN. *Collected Papers.* Edited by L. Oppenheim. Cambridge: University Press, 1914.

WHITE, A. D. *Seven Great Statesmen.* New York: Century, 1910.

WILSON, G. F. *International Law.* 8th ed. New York: Silver Burdett & Co., 1922.

WRIGHT, H. F. *Francisci de Victoria.* Washington: H. F. Wright, 1916.

WRIGHT, Q. *Mandates under the League of Nations.* Chicago: The University of Chicago Press, 1930.

ZIMMERN, A. *The Greek Commonwealth.* 4th ed. Oxford: Clarendon Press, 1924.

ARTICLES

ABBOTT, F. F. "Alberico Gentili and His Advocatio Hispanica", *American Journal of International Law*, X (1916), 737–748.

ADCOCK, F. E. "Some Aspects of Ancient Greek Diplomacy", *Proceedings of Classical Association of England and Wales*, XXI (1924), 92–116.

BALOGH, ELEMÉR. "The Traditional Element in Grotius' Conception of International Law", *New York University Law Quarterly Review*, VII (1930), 261–292.

BOAK, A. E. R. "Greek Interstate Associations and the League of Nations", *American Journal of International Law*, XV (1921), 375–383.

BRIÈRE, YVES DE LA. "La Conception de la Paix et de la Guerre chez Saint Augustin", *Revue de Philosophie*, Nouvelle Serie, I (1930), 557–572.

COLBY, ELBRIDGE. "How to Flight Savage Tribes", *American Journal of International Law*, XXI (1927), 279–288.

EAGLETON, CLYDE. "The Attempt to Define Aggression", *International Conciliation.* Nov. 1930, No. 264. New York: Carnegie Endowment for International Peace.

——. "The Attempt to Define War", *International Conciliation*, June 1933, No. 291. New York: Carnegie Endowment for International Peace.

FRANK, T. "The Import of the Fetial Institution", *Classical Philology*, VII (1912), 335–342.

GARDOT, ANDRÉ. "Jean Bodin, sa place parmi les fondateurs du droit international", *Hague. Académie de Droit International. Recueil des Cours* (Paris: Librairie du Recueil Sirey, 1935), L (1934), 545–747.

GEYL, PIETER. "Grotius", *Transactions of the Grotius Society*, XII (London: Sweet and Maxwell, 1927), 81–96.

GIDEL, GILBERT. "Droit et Devoirs des Nations", *Hague. Académie de Droit International. Recueil des Cours* (Paris: Libraire Hachette, 1927), X (1925), 541–597.

GOYAU, G. "L'Église Catholique et le Droit des Gens". *Hague. Académie du Droit International. Recueil des Cours* (Paris: Hachette, 1926), VI (1925), 127–236.

HAYES, C. H. "Truce of God", *Encyclopaedia Britannica*, XXII (14th ed.; New York: Encyclopaedia Britannica Inc., 1929), 506.

KELSEN, H. "Rechtstechnik und Abrüstung", *Der Deutsche Volkswirt*, VI (1932), 877–81.

KNIGHT, W. S. M. "Hugo Grotius", *Transactions of the Grotius Society*, VI (London: Sweet and Maxwell, 1920), 1–24.

KORFF, Baron S. A. "An Introduction to the History of International Law", *American Journal of International Law*, XVIII (1924), 246–259.

KREY, A. C. "International State of the Middle Ages", *American Historical Review*, XXVIII (1923), 1–12.

LAPRADELLE, ALBERT DE. "Introduction" in E. de Vattel, *Le Droit des Gens*, Vol. III. Washington: Carnegie Institution, 1916.

LARSON, J. A. O. "Was Greece Free between 196 and 146 B.C.?" *Classical Philology*, XXX (1935), 194–197.

LE FUR, L. "La Théorie du Droit Naturel depuis le XVIIe Siècle et la Doctrine Moderne". Hague. *Académie du Droit International. Recueil des Cours* (Paris: Hachette, 1928), XVIII (1927), 259–442.

LOUTER, J. DE. "Introduction" in C. van Bynkershoek, *Quaestionum Juris Publici Libri Duo*. Vol. II. Oxford: Clarendon Press, 1930.

MARTIN, W. A. P. "Traces of International Law in Ancient China", *International Review*, XIV (1883), 63–77.

MUNRO, D. C. "Speech of Pope Urban II", *American Historical Review*, XI (1906), 231–242.

NIPPOLD, O. "Introduction" in Christian Wolff's *Jus Gentium Methodo Scientifica Pertractatum*, Vol. II. Oxford: Clarendon Press, 1934.

NYS, E. "Introduction" in Franciscus de Victoria, *De Indis et De Jure Belli Relectiones*. Washington: Carnegie Institution, 1917.

PHILLIPSON, C. "Franciscus de Victoria", *Journal of Society of Comparative Legislation*, New Series, XV (1915), 175–97.

——. "Introduction" in Gentili, *De Jure Belli Libri Tres*, Vol. II. Oxford: Clarendon Press, 1933.

POUND, ROSCOE. "Grotius in the Science of Law", *American Journal International Law*, XIX (1925), 685–688.

RUTHERS, V. H. "La Mise en Harnonie du Pacte de la Société des Nations avec le Pacte de Paris", *Hague. Académie de Droit International. Recueil des Cours* (Paris: Libraire de Recueil Sirey, 1932), XXXVIII (1931), 5–27.

SCHUCKING, WALTHER. "Introduction" in Samuel von Pufendorf, *De Officio Hominis et Avis Juxta Legem Naturalem Libri Duo*, Vol. II. New York: Oxford University Press, 1927.

SCOTT, JAMES BROWN. "Grotius' De Jure Belli ac Pacis: The Work of a Lawyer, Statesman, and Theologian", *American Journal International Law*, XIX (1925), 461–468.

——. "Introduction" in C. van Bynkershoek, *De Dominio Maris Dissertatio*. New York: Oxford University Press, 1923.

SHERWOOD, F. W. "Francisco Suarez", *Transactions of the Grotius Society*, XII (1927), 19–28.

TRELLES, C. B. "Francisco Suarez", *Hague. Académie du Droit International. Recueil des Cours* (Paris: Libraire du Recueil Sirey, 1933), XLIII (1933), 389–546.

VAN VOLLENHOVEN, C. "Grotius and Geneva", *Bibliotheca Visseriana Dissertationum Jus-Internationale Illustrantium*, VI (Leyden: E. J. Brill, 1926), 1–8.

——. "Grotius and the Study of Law", *American Journal International Law*, XIX (1925), 1–11.

VON BAR, LUDWIG. "Introduction" in Johann Wolfgang Textor, *Synopsis Juris Gentium*, Vol. II. Washington: Carnegie Institution, 1916.

——. "Introduction" in Samuel Rachel, *De Jure Naturae et Gentium Dissertationes*, Vol. II. Washington, D. C.: Carnegie Institution, 1916.

WEHBERG, HANS. "Introduction" in Samuel von Pufendorf, *Elementorum Jurisprudentiae Universalis Libri Duo*, Vol. II. Oxford; Clarendon Press, 1931.

WEISS, ANDRÉ. "Le Droit Fétial et les Fétiaux à Rome", *La France*

Judiciaire (Paris: G. Pedone-Lauriel, 1883), Vol. III. No. 20, pp. 441–496.

WRIGHT, QUINCY. "Bombardment of Damascus", *American Journal of International Law*, XX (1926), 263–280.

——. "Changes in the Conception of War", *American Journal of International Law*, XVIII (1924), 755–767.

——. "Collective Rights and Duties for the Enforcement of Treaty Obligations", *Proceedings of American Society of International Law*, XXVI (1932), 101–119.

——. "The Concept of Aggression in International Law", *American Journal of International Law*, XXIX (1935), 372–395.

INDEX

Abelard, and just causes of war, 45

Ambrose, and just war, 42

Aristotle, and just causes of war, 19

Armed Neutrality of 1780, 137

Augustine: on declaration of war, 43; on just causes of war, 43; on just war, 41-2

Ayala: on declaration of war, 88, on distinction between peoples with respect to war, 88; on duty of third states, 90; on just war, 89; on whether or not war can be just on both sides, 89

Bacon: on distinction between peoples with respect to war, 75; favors war, 75; imperalism 77; on just causes of war, 76

Bartholomew de Las Casas, 62

Bodin: and nationalism, 105; similarity on war to Machiavelli, 66, note 1

Bonum commune of churchmen and legists, 102

Bryan treaties, and limitation on war with respect to time, 10

Bynkershoek: on declaration of war, 138-9; definition of war, 138; on distinction between peoples with respect to war, 138; on neutrality, 139-40

Charles V, 62

Cicero: on declaration of war, 28; on just causes of war, 28; on just war, 28

Colby, Captain Elbridge, and distinction between peoples with respect to war, 5

Conquistadores, 62

Cortez, 62

Council of Clermont, 34

Crusades, 34-6

Damascus, bombardemnt of, 4

Dante: and Holy Roman Emperor, 166; and settlement of disputes, 40, note 1

Declaration of war, 6, 14, 21–5, 35, 43, 62–3, 82, 88, 91, 95, 106, 111–2, 117–8, 121, 136, 138–9, 142–3, 147, 152–3; by herald, 63; by paper, 106

Decretum Gratiani, 45–6

Discoveries in the New World, 62

Distinction between peoples with respect to war, 4, 5, 13, 14, 18, 20, 21, 34, 72, 75, 79–81 88, 111, 120, 127, 136, 138

Duty of third states to go to war: 9, 90, 150

Egyptian Pharaohs and first treaties, 12

Eighteenth century: declaration of war in, 136; distinction between peoples, 136; frequency of wars in, 135; just cause of war, 136; just war, 136

Rerum repititio, 22
Rome: declaration of war in, 22–3; distinction between peoples in, 21; just war, 24–5; neutrality, 26; relations with foreigners, 20; truces, 26

Scott, James Brown: on Victoria, 78
Sino-Japanese dispute, 4
Suarez: on declaration of war, 91; on just causes of war, 92; on whether war can be just on both sides, 92

Textor: definition of war, 127; on distinction between peoples, 127; on just causes of war, 127–8; on neutrality, 130–1; similarity to Rachel, 126; on whether war can be just on both sides, 128–30
Thomas Aquinas: on just causes of war, 48; on just war, 47; and time limitations on war, 49
Time limitations on war, 9, 16, 26, 35, 37–9, 49, 150, 158
Truce of God, 37–9

Urban II, 34–5

Vattel: on declaration of war, 152–3; definition of international law, 151–2; on just causes of war, 154; on neutrality, 157; on proper motives for war, 154; on public war, 152; on offensive and defensive war, 153–4; relationship to Wolff, 150–1; on truces, 158; on whether war is just on both sides, 156
Victoria: on declaration of war, 82; on distinction between Indians and Spaniards, 79–81, on just causes of war; on just war, 83; on whether war can be just on both sides, 85–6

War, defined, 2, 94, 127, 138, 142
War, whether just on both sides, 85–6, 89, 92, 114, 128–30, 144, 149, 156
Wolff: *Civitas maxima*, 146; on declaration of war, 147; *jus gentium naturale*, 145; *jus gentium voluntarium*, 146; on just causes of war, 148–9; on neutrality, 149; on obligation of third states, 150; on offensive and defensive war, 147–8, on right of war, 146–7; on settlement of controversies through pacific means, 146; on truces, 150; on whether war can be just on both sides, 149
Wright, Quincy, and distinction between peoples, 4

Zouche: on declaration of war, 117–8; and *jus inter gentes*, 116; on just war, 118–9; significance in international law, 117